Cool It!

Cool It!

Teen Tips to Keep Hot Tempers from Boiling Over

Dr. Michael Hershorn

New Horizon Press
Far Hills, New Jersey

New Horizon Press
P.O. Box 669
Far Hills, NJ 07931

Michael Hershorn
      Cool It!: Teen Tips to Keep Hot Tempers from Boiling Over

Cover Design: Norma Erler Rahn
Interior Design: Susan M. Sanderson

Library of Congress Control Number: 2002103547

ISBN: 0-88282-230-6
New Horizon Press

Manufactured in the U.S.A.

2007   2006   2005   2004   2003   /   5   4   3   2   1

Author's Note

The material in this book is intended to provide an overview of methods and information now available. Any of the treatments described herein to manage or control anger should be discussed with a licensed health care/mental health practitioner. The author and publisher assume no responsibility for any adverse outcomes which derive from use of any of these treatments in a program of self-care or under the care of a licensed practitioner.

The information in this book is based on Michael Hershorn's research and practices with teenagers and their families. Fictitious identities and names have been given to individuals in this book. Some of the individuals in this book are composites of patients who participated in the author's research studies. For the purposes of simplifying usage, the pronouns his/him and her are often used interchangeably.

Table of Contents

Introduction

This book is for teenagers, all young adults between the ages of thirteen and nineteen. Some of you may be reading this book on your own initiative and that is great. Others may be reading this because you must. You may have gotten into trouble at school or with the police, or you may be having severe conflicts at home and someone else has bought this book and given it to you. A counselor may be requiring you to use this manual. Reading this book may be the last thing you feel like doing, but as long as you *are* reading it, you may as well try to get something out of it. I think you will.

I have worked with many angry teens who were brought to me by their parents to be "fixed." Some parents merely drop off their children and leave to run errands for the hour of their weekly "fix my kid" visit. Many teens resent this behavior, because it suggests that *they* are solely at fault and their parents are blame-free. Teens resent the idea that others think there is something wrong with them: "I'm not crazy. I don't need to be here. Why am I forced to be here?" If you have ever been in this situation, know that I understand. I do not work with crazy people. I work with men and women, young and old, who are experiencing problems in their lives. These problems may be perfectly understandable due to such causes as the chaotic world in which we live, divorce, stepparents, gang violence in schools and on the streets and drugs.

I know that the teens who come to me are not solely to blame for their problems. When parents drop off their kids at my office and want to run out, I try to get them to stay. Parents are often part of the problem as well. If parents never listen to their children, they never develop the skills to communicate and negotiate effectively. Your parents are often as confused as you are. They can get scared when their children grow up and demand independence. They may not know how to make the changes and allow their children to be heard rather than expecting them to listen. This failure may cause their children to explode with anger. In the end, this anger may be the catalyst which finally forces parents to let their offspring do whatever they want, often with disastrous consequences. Sometimes it takes years before old wounds can heal and adult children can establish good relationships with their parents.

So if someone in your family gave you this book, tell that person he or she should read it too. Your whole family should read it. All of you will need to work together, because the source of your anger problems does not lie with just one individual. Many of the tools and skills I will introduce will work better if your whole family understands and adopts them.

If your family is troubled, this book may help to calm some of those troubles. Many times parents lay all blame for the family's problems at the feet of their children. They do this because it feels safer to send their children for help than to acknowledge that they might have problems as well. Problems in a marriage can often be the underlying cause of a child's anger problems. There can be arguments. There can be inconsistency and chaos. Kids can be pushed by one parent and pulled by the other. Kids are sometimes given the job of drawing attention away from unspeakable problems: a parent's alcoholism, an unhappy marriage, a messy divorce and lingering resentment. I hope that reading this book will help you change your thoughts about your family. Remember what I said before: you are not the whole problem. You are not crazy. You may be able to help yourself and some others too. You can feel good about that.

Unfortunately, there are times when parents and other family members will not participate. Some divorced parents cannot even stand to be in the same room together. When this is the case, I work just with the kids. I work with them to help them deal with a bad situation. You shouldn't be in the hot seat or in trouble. You've probably tried and failed to get yourself out of the spotlight. We can work together to get you out of that bad place. Use this book to help yourself and your friends. I know many teenagers who get more help from their friends than anyone else. Whole groups of friends enter counseling together and help each other to handle their problems more constructively. Be the agent of change for yourself and your friends.

There is something else in all of this for you personally. Most teens want more freedom or trust or more realistic expectations from their parents. By taking control of the only thing you can really change—yourself— you will find these goals within your reach. If you cool your anger, find some new ways to express yourself and learn both how to give a little and get a little, your life will change in concrete ways. For example, you may learn how to stay out of trouble at school or with the police. Or how to stay out of fights. Or how to get along better with girlfriends or boyfriends. Or how to avoid being picked on. The people around you will become more trusting, and with trust comes more freedom. Think positively about what you will gain by working on yourself and resolving your anger problems.

This book will teach you a lot about the anger you are feeling and how you can better manage it. There will be exercises for you to perform and new skills to practice. This practice helps you change the way you process anger and use this knowledge when you are out in the real world. Together we'll go over actual case histories of teens I have helped in order to illustrate the various points we're discussing. In addition, I hope these histories will remind you that you are not alone and inspire you to change as well. Many of you will be able to relate to these teenagers because you will find aspects of your own experiences reflected in their stories. Please note that I have changed all names, along with some minor details, in order to protect my clients' confidentiality. However, I have written about them with their full knowledge and permission. All of my clients were enthusiastic about having their stories told. They felt good that their stories of coping with anger might help others. Helping others will often cement one's own changes. When people change, they begin with anger, guilt, shame and remorse and end with overwhelming feelings of relief and well-being.

So let's embark on a journey together. Let's figure this thing out as partners. Open up to yourself and take an honest look inside. Don't judge yourself. Instead, look to understand the reasons for your anger and find solutions to your problems. Discover that you've got a great chance to succeed in handling your angry feelings in new, positive ways.

part 1

Teen Emotions Defined

chapter 1

You Are Not Alone

...all this commotion,
emotions running deep as ocean's explodin',
tempers flaring from parents,
just blow 'em off and keep goin'...
- Eminem, "Cleaning Out My Closet"

Before we begin discussing how you can manage your anger, I'd like to spend this chapter introducing you to some teens I've helped in my counseling sessions. You may find their problems similar to your own. While you are reading these stories, I hope you will feel inspired by my patients' desire to change. Remember: if they could learn to control their anger, so can you.

TONY

Tony was sixteen years old when he first came to see me. He was big and had the appearance of being a tough guy. He came to my office with his father after his second suspension from high school for fighting. One more suspension and he would be expelled. Tony's parents had divorced several years ago. When he was younger, Tony had lived with his mother in a low income neighborhood. His high school there was a tough one, where gangs fought on a daily basis. Tony and his friends had a tough reputation and other kids knew not to mess with them.

Back when Tony lived with his mom, the two did not get along well. He thought his mother didn't respect him and always seemed disappointed with him. She could not really control him because of his size, so they had frequent yelling matches. Tony also had a lot of anger about his parents' divorce. He seemed to wish that he still had an intact family with two parents who could assign him boundaries. Before the divorce, Tony had been involved in football and wrestling. After the divorce, he gave up sports and spent his free time hanging out with an older group of kids.

Because Tony's mom couldn't control her son, she and her ex-husband decided that Tony should move in with his father at the start of the school year. Tony's dad was a big guy, so Tony gave him more respect than he did his mom and thus there was less conflict at home. When the two of them were seen together, Tony and his dad seemed more like friends than father and son. I suspected that his dad had fewer expectations of Tony than his mom did. Tony's dad confirmed this to be true when he said his ex was "over-emotional about things;" he told me that was one of the reasons why he had left her. Tony probably had been getting mixed messages from his parents: his mom wanted him to be more of a child, while his dad wanted him to be more of an adult.

Another problem that presented itself was that Tony's dad moved to a more affluent town after the divorce. When Tony moved in with his dad, he had to change high schools. This had been part of the plan—to get Tony away from what his parents saw as "bad" influences. But Tony did not fit in as well in this new school. He was frequently challenged by other kids who wanted to mess with the new tough guy. Tony told me that when other kids challenged him, he would just "go off" and pound them. I guessed that these fights did not last very long.

In time, this tough new student earned a bad reputation with the teachers and administrators. They began to scrutinize him more and more closely. It didn't matter that he had never actually started a fight. Tony thought this treatment was unfair and felt very frustrated with the situation and with himself. He did care about school and did not want to be expelled. Although he did not come to counseling by choice, he was motivated to change. As long as he had to come in, he decided to work on controlling his anger and eliminating the need to fight.

I didn't find it necessary to see Tony very many times. Our talks helped him figure out that when he got angry, he should not simply "go off" without cause or control. He saw that he was still angry from his parents' divorce and that this influenced his behavior. He also came to see that there was always a moment between being challenged to a fight by another student and deciding to take that challenge when Tony could gain control of himself. Tony learned to notice his anger before it became too strong to handle. He learned how to calm himself down. Being calmer, Tony was able to decide that he did not have to fight. Soon the uproar over this new student died down. The other students lost interest in challenging him. The administrators appreciated that Tony's dad had brought him for counseling.

Tony also started venting about the true sources of his anger. He had been walking around with those feelings locked inside himself, unable to share them with anyone. He resented the fact that his dad had left. He was angry that his mom yelled at *him* now that she could no longer yell at his dad. He realized that fighting had been his only way of releasing his angry feelings. The more he talked to me, the less his anger persisted. That is very natural. If you can talk about your negative feelings, you are a lot less likely to act on them. We had some sessions where Tony was able to tell his dad how angry he was about the divorce. He also told his dad that he needed him to be a father, not a friend. He felt they shouldn't be two buddies who swapped war stories about how mom was so over-reactive and emotional. Tony didn't want to hear his dad put down his mom.

Tony was satisfied that he had changed his behavior. He had released his anger and gotten his dad to understand him. He started participating in sports again. He used exercise rather than fighting to release his stress, especially the stress he felt when visiting his mother. I'm proud to say that our work was a success—Tony was never suspended from school again.

JENNIFER

Jennifer was a seventeen-year-old high school senior when she came to see me. She was intelligent and popular. She was very excited about all the events of her last year in high school. She had been accepted to a good college and was both happy and nervous about going there. As it happened, her older sister already attended the college where Jennifer had been accepted. The two of them were close and got along well. Jennifer was looking forward to joining her sister.

Jennifer was active in cheerleading and worked part-time after school. She had not yet had a serious relationship with a boy. Her friends were among the most popular, wealthy and attractive girls at school. Although she was also attractive, Jennifer felt she had to work hard to keep up with her friends in the looks department. On the surface, this is what led to her problem. Jennifer came to counseling, because her parents and friends were very concerned about her weight loss. She was concerned as well and wanted help, but was too ashamed to ask for it herself.

Jennifer had started out wanting to lose some weight. She did this on her own by eating less and working out more. The problem was that her dieting began to spiral out of control. She could not stop losing weight. She became obsessed with counting calories and exercising. No matter how much weight she lost, she still thought that she looked too heavy in the mirror. Jennifer knew in her head that this was not rational, but she couldn't change how she felt. If the scale did not show a steady decrease in weight, she would panic. If she gained even a pound, Jennifer feared that she would soon gain back all of her weight. Again, she knew that this was not rational, but she couldn't stop herself. In truth, Jennifer had not been overweight when she had started dieting. But she thought her friends all had perfect figures and that this was why they had boyfriends and she didn't. She liked herself better after she had lost ten pounds. Soon she had lost twenty pounds and wanted to keep going. This frightened her. Her family and friends became concerned about her appearance. People thought she had some terrible illness, because she had become so thin. All of this had occurred within the span of six months.

Many of you may know about eating disorders such as anorexia and bulimia. They can be very serious and deadly. Patients who suffer from these disorders must usually be hospitalized when their weight drops below seventy or eighty pounds. Jennifer knew all about this, as did her parents. They took the problem seriously by seeking help for their daughter early on. A medical checkup and blood test confirmed that Jennifer was not binging and purging (throwing up or taking too many laxatives). After taking her to the doctor, Jennifer's parents decided to take her to see me.

I gave Jennifer more information about eating disorders. Together we worked on getting her to stop over-exercising, weighing herself daily and constantly examining herself in the mirror. We worked on having her recognize and dispel irrational thoughts about herself and her weight. I also referred Jennifer to a nutritionist to work on a meal plan and to a trainer to change her work-out routine.

Jennifer's parents accompanied her at her counseling sessions. As it turned out, Jennifer's mom was also obsessive about her weight. Her mom weighed herself everyday as well—that's where Jennifer learned *that* habit. Her mom also worked out almost daily. During our sessions together, I tried to find in Jennifer's family history some of the more common issues that can cause eating disorders. But this proved fruitless, because Jennifer didn't relate to any of my suggestions. Sometimes teens can develop eating disorders in reaction to an overly-controlling parent—food becomes the thing that the teen can secretly control. However, this was not the case with Jennifer.

What I did discover was that the parents were going through a marital crisis. Jennifer's dad was becoming more and more distant from the family. Jennifer often came home to hear her parents arguing. Whenever this happened, she turned around and left without her parents even knowing she had been there. Sometimes at night she heard them argue as she lay in bed; she buried her head in the pillows and sobbed quietly.

Jennifer came to realize that her obsession with weight loss was related to problems within her family, particularly her parents' marital crisis. Focusing on her weight distracted her from her feelings of anger and despair over their arguments. She did not even know she had these feelings until she discovered them in counseling. Therapy also helped bring her dad back into the picture. Before the marital crisis, Jennifer and her dad had been close and often had good, meaningful talks about everything going on in their lives. Jennifer needed her dad to pay attention to her again. She also needed her mom not to lean on her daughter so heavily for support.

It was not easy for Jennifer to acknowledge the anger she felt toward her parents, particularly her father. She found it unacceptable to be angry with them. "I'm not supposed to be angry with my parents," she said. I asked Jennifer to keep a journal and be honest when writing down her feelings. She was not one for expressing herself to others—she needed a private outlet. In time, she used our sessions together as another outlet to confess her true feelings.

Eventually, our talks helped Jennifer to express her feelings directly to her mother and father. This prompted her parents to enter counseling as well, both individually and together as a couple. By dealing with her own problem, Jennifer had gotten her family the help it needed. Once her family addressed the real problems, Jennifer could let go of her own. She soon left for college. Her school had a special clinic for eating disorders; this clinic diagnosed Jennifer as not having a true eating disorder, but just some aspects of an eating disorder. Jennifer is now in individual counseling and sees a nutritionist regularly. Her weight remains at a stable level. She expresses her feelings better now than before and knows that she can be a good person even when she feels anger toward others.

Over a year after I stopped seeing her, Jennifer called to give me an update on how she was doing. She had joined a sorority at school. As it happened, one of her sorority sisters was suffering from an extreme eating problem. Jennifer said her friend looked like an "alien with an emaciated body and a large head." When Jennifer had tried to help her, she was rebuffed. The girl said, "Yes, I know I have to eat," just to get people off her back. Before Thanksgiving break, the girl told Jennifer that she was afraid that eating Thanksgiving dinner would make her fat. Jennifer was overwhelmed by her confession and became deeply concerned. Although Jennifer had revealed her own problems with weight loss to her friend, nothing was getting through. Others were getting nowhere, too. Jennifer asked me to help her brainstorm for possible solutions to the problem. We decided that Jennifer should go to the president of the sorority with her concerns. School medical authorities would have to be involved, because the girl was in a life-or-death situation. We also talked about how it would be wrong for Jennifer to assume too much responsibility for her friend. It would be enough for Jennifer to get her friend into the hands of the medical and mental health professionals at the school. I pointed out to Jennifer that she had done an about-face: once she looked to others for help, but now she was in a position to help others.

JAMES

James was fifteen when he came to see me. He was discovered to be drunk at school and was sent to a special school counselor who dealt with substance abuse. The counselor offered him a choice: either accept a ten-day suspension or come to counseling with me. After consulting with his dad, James chose therapy instead of the suspension.

James' dad brought him to my office. James was pleasant about the fact that he had been forced into therapy, but he thought he was not the problem. He happened to be exactly right. His family problems were serious and James was justifiably angry about them; however, James created his own problems by dealing with his anger in very self-destructive ways. He would often get drunk with friends both at school and away from school. He allowed his grades to drop from As and Bs to Ds and Fs. In years past, James had excelled in league sports, but now he had dropped out of sports completely. James told me he was not going to try out for his school's baseball team, despite having been a league all-star for years.

James' parents had recently divorced. His mom was an alcoholic who drank far too frequently. James' dad had tried to stop her from drinking but failed; eventually, he grew tired of dealing with the problem and divorced her. After the split, James' dad kept their family home while James moved with his brother and his mom to a townhouse only a couple of miles away. The two parents split visitation rights equally between them, with the boys spending half the week with one parent and half with the other.

James told me he preferred living with his mom, because he got along better with her. James and his dad clashed a lot. His dad had many rules and regulations, such as expecting James to be home at a certain time, demanding that he stay away from certain friends, ordering him to keep up with some responsibilities around the house and so on. Dad would often harshly criticize James right to his face. James thought his dad was a control freak and sometimes he got so angry at him that he could hardly speak. When that happened, James just threw his hands up in the air and stuttered some half-sentences, while his dad continued on with a barrage of criticism. When this happened during our therapy sessions, I put a stop to it by telling James' dad that he was there not just to talk but also to listen. By playing referee, I kept James' dad from turning our sessions into a "James-bashing" exercise. When James saw me in sessions without his dad, he expressed a lot of anger and hostility toward his father.

When James and his brother were at their mom's house, she gave them a lot of freedom. She had no expectations of James and pretty much allowed him to do whatever he wanted. However, it also seemed that his mother wanted James to replace her husband and become her caretaker. She was a binge drinker who had been in and out of several alcohol-treatment programs. She stayed sober for a few days and then get completely drunk. In one of our sessions, James told me that he and his brother tried to watch over their mom. His younger brother's job was to make sure that mom took her Antabuse pills, which are sometimes prescribed for alcoholics who are out of control. They cause violent nausea in a person whenever he or she consumes alcohol. However, alcoholics who want to continue drinking simply stop taking the pills. I remarked to James that it seemed like too much responsibility for a ten-year-old to make sure his mom took her pills. James agreed and said that he would take over this chore. I told James that this was too much responsibility for a fifteen-year-old as well. He nodded glumly and seemed to get my point.

James was caught in a terrible bind, because he lived in two extreme situations. On the one hand, his mom gave him complete freedom to do whatever he liked but also saddled him with responsibilities that he was too young to handle. On the other hand, his dad acted like a real parent toward him but controlled and criticized him to death. At first, James directed all his anger toward his dad. He felt too responsible for his mother to allow himself to be angry about her drinking. He also had no day-to-day conflicts with her, because she gave him complete freedom.

James' confusion could be seen most clearly in his attitude toward his own drinking. Despite all of the drug education provided in his school, James thought his own drinking was okay. Despite the fact that he knew that he was more likely to become an alcoholic because of his mother's alcoholism, James denied that this could ever be a problem for him. He saw the problems that alcohol had caused in his mother's daily life, but could not see them in his own. James drank to escape and to repress feelings of anger toward his mother that he could not consciously acknowledge.

Although James' father was the only functioning parent in the picture, he was far too extreme in his control and criticism to do the job effectively. James and his dad were locked in a vicious cycle that only made them angrier with each other and made them grow farther apart. I found it interesting that James had given up baseball, because his dad had played minor league baseball. Obviously James was trying to get back at his dad, but his behavior was hurting himself as well.

Through our talks, James accepted that his mom's drinking was neither his nor his dad's responsibility. I helped James' father to work on his parenting skills and become less controlling and critical. James and his dad learned how to communicate and cooperate together. In time, James began to take less responsibility for his mom and allowed himself to feel his anger over her drinking. He started going to Al-Ateen meetings, which are support group meetings for teens who deal with an alcoholic parent. James stopped drinking entirely and had no more drunken episodes at school. His grades shot back up and he grew eager to try out for the baseball team at school.

I have shared these real life stories to give you a feel for the kinds of difficulties with anger other teens have faced and conquered. I also want you to become aware how unexpressed, misdirected or extreme anger can lead to other serious problems. Now we can work together on how to deal with the anger you are feeling and find positive ways to resolve it.

Teen Anger Tips

- If you are being forced to read this book against your will, stick with it anyway. Together we can resolve your anger problem.
- Remember: you are not crazy. You are not the whole problem.
- Be open to changing how you express and handle your anger.
- Ask all your family members to read this book. Tell them that I said they should.
- Take control of the only thing you can control: **Yourself**.
- You can earn more trust and freedom from your family by getting them to have more realistic expectations about you.

chapter 2

Feelings and Anger

...I'm blowin' comin' up inside
like the Bee Gees cry I'm just stayin' alive...
- Saliva, "Your Disease"

Emotions are a part of being human. Because anger is a normal human emotion, it's perfectly normal for us to feel angry at times. No one is ever wrong for feeling anger. The important thing is what we do with our anger and how we express it. We can express our anger in either healthy or unhealthy ways.

The first lesson in anger management is that it is okay to be angry. Everybody feels angry at some time or other, so why deny it? In the past, I've been required to evaluate applicants for law-enforcement jobs. When I did, I always asked them to answer whether the following statement was true or false: "Sometimes I feel so angry I could break something." Because the candidates wanted to give the best possible impressions of themselves, they would invariably respond "false," even though they knew the correct answer for them was "true." Of course, this is natural for people looking for a job—they always want to create a good impression. But it is also natural for people to feel so angry at times that they just want to break something. I didn't ask the applicants if they actually *had* broken something—only if they had *wanted* to. Remember that there is a big difference between thinking something and acting on it.

Anger may be a normal human emotion, but we must be very careful in how we express that anger. In this book, we will work together so that you express your angry feelings in words, not actions. Many of us have learned to express anger in destructive ways, but these habits can be unlearned. This book will discuss ways to manage your anger within the first moments of feeling it. With practice, you will achieve the ultimate goal of expressing anger calmly in words. By doing so, you will be able to resolve the conflict quickly, make yourself understood and feel better about yourself.

Dr. Ah: Four Steps to Anger Management

Many people have told me that I seem to be a laid-back kind of guy. In fact, I've worked hard at learning how to be relaxed and calm. I've become so laid-back, you might say that my nickname is "Dr. Ah." Let "Dr. Ah" teach you how to relax as well.

Use the letters in **Dr. Ah** to help you remember the four easy steps to managing your anger. Those steps are:

1) **D**ecide to make a commitment.
2) **R**ecognize your anger cues, signs or signals.
3) **A**ctivate the relaxation response.
4) **H**alt. Take a Time Out.

Let's examine each of these steps one by one. The **"D"** stands for "**D**ecide to make a commitment." By reading this book, you have already begun to commit to change. If you are reading this book only because someone has forced you to, make the best of it. Seize this opportunity to make a change for the better. If you do this now, no one will ever tell you to do something about your anger again. When I work with people who have anger management problems, I always ask them to make a commitment to change. I want you to do the same thing now. Make a promise to change and write it down here:

_____

_____

_____

Now that you have committed yourself to change, I want you to keep reading this book even when you have more fun things to do. Make sure you complete all the exercises that follow. Complete them fully—don't just skim over them and say to yourself, "Oh, I get the idea. I don't actually have to do that." I am trying to help you change behaviors and habits that you've learned and repeated over the whole course of your life. This change takes time and won't happen unless you make a complete effort, so do everything I ask you to! Don't worry—the exercises won't take very long and you'll find that they're worth the effort.

After the "D" in "Dr. Ah" comes **"R,"** which stands for "**R**ecognizing your anger cues, signs or signals." When people explode in a fit of anger, they often explain their behavior by saying: "I just snapped...I lost control...I just went off...I totally lost it." But is this really an accurate way to describe what happens when we get angry? Think about yourself for a minute. When you've gotten angry, have you ever *completely* lost control?

No doubt there's been a time when you've gotten angry with someone in a position of authority. When that happened, did you...
> ...Tackle that person to the ground and pummel him nearly to death?
> ...Tear her office apart?
> ...Scream at the top of your lungs?
> ...Use the foulest language known to humankind?

Sometime in your life, you may have hit a friend or sibling. When that happened, did you...
> ...Hit him as hard as you possibly could?
> ...Use a blunt object instead of your hands?
> ...Continue hitting until that person lost consciousness?

Perhaps there's been a time when you've been hassled by the cops. When that happened, did you...
> ...Physically attack the officer?
> ...Go for the officer's gun?
> ...Threaten the officer's life?
> ...Pound on the officer's patrol car?

Every kid has had the experience of being dissed by a classmate at school. When that happened to you, did you...
> ...Smash your classmate's head in?
> ...Go to your classmate's house and smash in all of her windows?

Most likely, your answer to all of these questions was "NO." This is important, because it shows that although you may lose *some* control when you get angry, you do not lose *complete* control. The questions I posed were actions that you *might have taken* in certain situations, but instead *chose not to*. Thus you still control yourself even when acting out in anger. This is good news. If you are able to exercise some control during your angry moments, you can learn how to exercise even more control.

Once you learn that you exercise control even when you are angry, you can learn to recognize the onset of anger before it strikes. Anger is not a matter of simply "going off" or "snapping." There are always early warning signs to anger. When you learn to recognize these signs, you will be on guard against your anger and thus better able to control it. The warning signs can be classified into four major groups: sensations, actions, thoughts and feelings. Let's discuss them one at a time.

SENSATIONS

Here are some physical sensations that can signal the beginning of an anger attack:

- ◆ Face flushing
- ◆ Quickened heart beat
- ◆ Heart pounding
- ◆ The feeling of blood rushing through your veins
- ◆ Feeling hot
- ◆ Muscles tensing

ACTIONS

We are not always consciously aware of all our actions. Here are some unconscious actions that, if you become aware you are doing them, might tip you off that you are about to lose your temper:

- ◆ Pacing
- ◆ Restlessness
- ◆ Inability to sit still
- ◆ Clenching of fists or jaw
- ◆ Talking more rapidly or loudly than usual
- ◆ Punching one's hand
- ◆ Leg bobbing

THOUGHTS

Oftentimes, certain thoughts are clues that you're close to exploding:

- ◆ *She's doing this purposely to piss me off.*
- ◆ *This has been a bad day. I've got to let off some steam.*
- ◆ *I look like a fool in front of everybody.*
- ◆ *He's intentionally trying to hurt me.*

FEELINGS

Of course, the feeling of anger itself is a clear sign that you are in danger of becoming enraged. However, there are many feelings that may precede an anger attack. Some might include:

- ◆ Insecurity
- ◆ Confusion
- ◆ Hurt
- ◆ Sorrow
- ◆ Annoyance

These are all examples of early warning signs that signal a possible anger attack. If you learn to recognize these signals in time, you will be able to stop yourself before you explode. Take a moment and think of your own early warning signs. Which of the signs that we've discussed do *you* feel when you are about to become angry? Do you have warning signs that haven't been listed here? Write down all your anger signs in the space that follows. Doing this will help you to remember your anger signals and recognize them when they surface. We will discuss this subject in greater detail in chapter 6.

MY ANGER WARNING SIGNS

1. _____
2. _____
3. _____
4. _____
5. _____

Let's return to "Dr. Ah." The **"A"** stands for **"Activating relaxation."** The idea here is to relax yourself the very moment you recognize your anger warning signs. The state of relaxation blocks anger. Science has shown that it is impossible for your body to be both relaxed and angry at the same time; therefore, if you relax, you will drive away anger. Once you recognize one or two of the early warning signs we've discussed, you should activate relaxation. The earlier you intervene, the easier it will be to shift from anger to relaxation. Many of you may already use relaxation methods for other reasons; use them to keep yourself from acting out in anger as well. You can also use such relaxing activities as taking a walk, bicycling, working out, taking a shower, lying down, reading a book or magazine, watching television, listening to music, breathing deeply, praying or meditating. Choose whatever relaxing activity best suits you. When you perform this activity, it is important to focus on the relaxation and not brood about whatever made you angry. Your goal is to get your mind off your anger and relax.

Let me give you some quick relaxation techniques that you can use whenever you feel angry. The first technique requires you to sit or lie down in a comfortable position. Breathe in through your nose and out through your mouth. As you breathe in, say **"calm"** to yourself and, as you breathe out, say **"peace."** Do this rhythmically in tune with your breathing.

The second method focuses on muscle tension. Take notice of any tension in any of the muscle groups in your body and relax the tension away. The major muscle groups in your body are in your head and face, your neck, your shoulders, your arms and hands, your chest, your stomach, your upper and lower back, your butt, your thighs, your calves and your feet and toes. Start with the muscles of your head and imagine the tension there simply draining from your body. Slowly work down through all the muscles of your body until your reach your toes. If you prefer, you might imagine that the chair or bed underneath you is a giant sponge absorbing the tension out of your body. Check in with each part of your body and release any tension by relaxing those muscles. Notice the difference between the bad feelings of tension and the good feelings of relaxation. Again, start at the top of your head and work down to your toes.

A third technique is a variation of the one just described. In this exercise, you will also work down your body as you did before, but this time you will purposely tense the muscles in each major group for a three count and then relax them for a five count. Notice the tension as you tighten and hold your muscles. Then notice the tension drain away as you release and relax your muscles. Doing this will train you to become aware of muscle tension more quickly. The quicker you can notice tension, the faster you can intervene and relax it away. We all walk around with muscle tension during the day and do not even realize it. Many of us hold tension in particular places like the neck and shoulders. If you can become aware of this tension and dispel it immediately, you will reduce stress and become less likely to feel irritated or become angry. You will also increase your sense of calm and well-being, because if your body feels at ease, your spirit will feel at ease as well.

Our fourth relaxation exercise involves the use of imagery. Close your eyes and imagine yourself in an actual place where you once visited and felt at peace. Use all of your senses to create this place in your mind. For example, imagine yourself lying on a sandy beach you once visited. Feel the sand beneath the blanket perfectly cradling your body. Feel the warm sun on your skin and a cooling breeze blowing over you, keeping your temperature just right. Hear the sounds of the waves rolling onto the shore, the wind as it rustles through the dune grass and the seagulls off in the distance. See the blue sky, the white clouds and the gulls as they circle overhead. See the long expanse of white beach and the waves rolling on the shoreline. Look to the horizon and notice where the ocean meets the sky. Notice the difference between the blue-green of the ocean and the blue of the sky. Smell the salty sea air as you breathe in and out. Taste the salt in the air on your tongue. This is an example of how you can use all your senses to imagine yourself in a relaxing place. See, feel, hear, smell and even taste the things around you. You can use your imagination to return to this place whenever you need to and whenever you want to. Pretend that you are taking a mini-vacation during the middle of the day. Doing so will keep your general level of tension down. The more you practice this exercise, the easier these images will come to you.

A fifth technique asks you to make suggestions to yourself. When we are relaxed, we become more receptive and open to change. This exercise is like self-hypnosis and is nothing more than getting relaxed and making positive suggestions to ourselves. For example, you might think to yourself:

I will let this anger go.

I will focus on what is good and not on what is bad.

I will express my anger in words.
I will practice relaxation as soon as I notice anger signs.

Use all of these relaxation techniques to help you reduce anger. Feel free to mix and match them. Use different combinations of these exercises to develop your own personal relaxation method. Using these techniques will help you break the vicious cycle of feeling, thinking and acting with relaxation. We will return to this subject and discuss it in greater detail when we get to chapter 8.

Now let's move on to the final letter of "Dr. Ah." The **"H"** stands for **"Halt."** This means you should take a Time Out from any situation that causes you to get angry. By removing yourself from an angry situation, you give yourself the chance to calm down and deal with the problem later in a more constructive way. You may need more than one Time Out in the same situation. As you notice anger cues, call a Time Out as often as you need in order to avoid acting out in anger. Use a relaxation technique during your Time Out. Return to the situation only when you are calm enough to address any problems or conflicts with the other person. Make sure that you do return, so the other person won't feel "blown off." If the other person sees that you are not simply avoiding the situation, he or she will trust the Time Out technique in the future.

There may be times when it would not be appropriate to leave the room for a Time Out. When dealing with a principal, teacher or police officer, for example, it's better to simply announce a Time Out to yourself in your head. In these cases, imagine yourself in a relaxing place and practice a relaxation skill like rhythmic breathing.

You should be sure to explain the concept of the Time Out beforehand to your family and friends. Don't wait until you become angry to explain why you are suddenly leaving the room during an argument. Tell your loved ones that they may call a Time Out as well; however, explain that they may only call a Time Out for themselves and never for another person. Ultimately, we only have control over ourselves. If we tell someone else to take a Time Out, that person may resent being ordered around. The Time Out may then become the focus of the argument. Each person should take responsibility for noticing his/her own anger and calling his/her own Time Out. That person should walk out of the room and engage in a relaxing activity.

Let the Time Out last for anywhere from a few minutes to an hour, but don't let it go on much longer than that. Extremely long Time Outs become too much like two people not talking to each other after an argument. The other person needs to know that when you take a Time Out, you will return when ready. Remember that Time Outs are personal time—the other person should not interrupt or attempt to end the Time Out in any way. Once the Time Out is over, all parties should return to the matter at hand and try to resolve the issue. If you feel your anger building a second time, feel free to take a second Time Out. Always take a Time Out calmly—don't slam doors or sneak in a few last words on your way out. Simply stop everything and go off to relax. If you are in a car, stop discussion completely. You might put on the radio or engage in a relaxation technique.

Practice calling for a Time Out with your parents when everyone is still calm. This kind of role-play will help everyone understand how a Time Out works and what he/she is meant to do. Practicing beforehand will make the Time Out work better in the heat of the moment.

If you learn to call a Time Out whenever you need it, you will be able to dispel your anger before it becomes destructive. You can say goodbye to detentions, suspensions and arrests. More importantly, you will no longer suffer from the tension of anger or the guilt of having acted out in anger. I know that when I let something go, I feel good about myself. Make sure that you notice your own good feelings whenever you manage your anger successfully. These good feelings will reinforce your changed behavior and encourage you to act similarly the next time. We will return to the subject of the Time Out and discuss it in greater detail in chapter 7. Ask your parents to read this section and chapter 7 to be sure they understand the Time Out concept.

Before we end this chapter, let's review the four steps to anger management. You can remember these steps with the four letters of **Dr. Ah**: **D**ecide to commit. **R**ecognize your anger signs. **A**ctivate your relaxation response. **H**alt and call a Time Out. **Dr. Ah**: **D**ecide, **R**ecognize, **A**ctivate, **H**alt. That's all you need to remember to keep your anger under control. The rest of this book will expand on these ideas and teach you even more skills to help you manage your anger successfully.

Teen Anger Tips

- ◆ Feeling anger is normal.
- ◆ Problems occur only when we act out in anger.
- ◆ Consult with Dr. Ah.
- ◆ Remember the four steps to managing your anger: **D**ecide to commit, **R**ecognize cues, **A**ctivate relaxation and **H**alt.
- ◆ Use these four steps to enable you to dispel your anger before it becomes a problem.
- ◆ Continue reading this book to reinforce these changes and learn new anger management techniques.

part II

Teen Anger Strategies

chapter 3

When Anger Leads to Problems

I hate you. I hate you – shut up…
You think that I'm the one to blame.
Everything I lose is just a piece of what there is to gain…
-Ill Nino, "What Comes Around"

Anger may have had an important survival value for our primitive ancestors. The adrenaline rush, the tunnel vision, the rapid heart beat, the flow of blood to the extremities probably made those "cavemen" better fighters or hunters. However, in modern society this "fight or flight" response is no longer valuable. You can be arrested for angry acts resulting in violence. If you cannot check your anger, you will destroy your relationships with others and ultimately destroy yourself. However, if you cannot express your anger at all, you may develop ulcers, headaches, back and neck pain, anxiety, panic and depression. Bottling up anger is not the solution either. What we need to do is find a middle course between these two extremes. We need to find a way to deal with our anger without holding it in and without acting destructively.

Before we continue, let me make an important distinction between **expressing anger in words and expressing anger in actions.**

Calmly stating "I feel angry right now because…" is the healthiest, most constructive way to express angry feelings. Using words and not actions will make it more likely that the other person will understand what you are feeling and will respond accordingly. If you deal with your anger this way, things will go more smoothly. You will be able to work the problem out. The positive reinforcement of verbalizing your feelings will make it more likely that you'll resort to words and not actions the next time you get angry. It will become easier to respond to an anger-provoking situation by saying:

"I feel angry now because...."

Remember that not all verbal expressions deal with anger constructively. Cursing, shouting, name-calling and put-downs have more in common with acting out in anger than with saying how you feel. Expressing yourself this way can hurt others, sometimes even more so than physical aggression can. It is said that emotional scars last much longer than physical ones.

My research has shown that different people lose control of their anger in different ways. When people see me for help, I usually tailor my counseling sessions to address that person's individual way of dealing with his or her anger. There is no one way to deal with every situation. Help needs to be specific for different types of anger problems. I've found that these anger problems fall into three broad categories: anger internalization, over-controlled anger and under-controlled anger. As you read on, you will find yourself falling into one of these three categories.

The first category is **anger internalization**. This category describes people who keep their emotions bottled up. For whatever reason, these people have strong internal controls that keep them from ever expressing their anger. As a result, they become passive. Because they cannot release their anger in any way, they become sick from it. This is what is meant when we say that anger is "turned against the self." People who internalize their anger get ulcers, headaches, pain, depression, anxiety and panic attacks. They may also express their anger by purposefully *not* saying or doing something. They intentionally withhold what others ask of them in order to get back at them. This is called being "passive-aggressive."

The second category is **over-controlled anger**. Like internalizers, the people in this category also have strong controls against the expression of anger. However, these people eventually do release their anger. They allow their anger to build and build until some minor event finally triggers an intense, explosive outburst. This outburst is usually short in duration and causes the person to feel guilt and remorse afterwards. People who suffer from over-controlled anger usually direct their rage at objects that cannot fight back—"safe" targets such as inanimate objects or younger siblings.

The last category is **under-controlled anger**. This category describes people who have few controls against the expression of anger. Their outbursts occur more frequently but are less intense and can be directed at any number of objects, including friends, bosses, teachers, strangers, significant others and even police. Please note that these three categories are not absolute. Sometimes people can share traits of more than one category at a time.

In the pages that follow, you will find some tests that will measure how well you are able to manage your anger. Take the tests now and then take them again sometime in the future in order to chart your success. If you practice the skills introduced in this book, you will see your scores on these tests improve. This will be a mark of your progress.

Test #1:
When is Your Anger a Problem?

At some point in our lives, everyone experiences unjustified and unnecessary anger. However, if this happens too often, it can lead to problems. Here are a few signs that will tell you when your anger is creating problems for you.

1. *When it is too frequent.* There are many situations for which being angry is justified and proper. However, we often get angry even when it is not necessary or useful. You need to make a distinction between the times when it is alright to be angry and when getting angry isn't such a good idea.

2. *When it is too intense.* Anger is something that occurs at different levels of intensity. A small or moderate amount of anger can often work to your advantage. But a high degree of anger seldom produces positive results.

3. *When it lasts too long.* When you prolong your anger, your body must maintain a level of arousal or stress that goes beyond normal limits. We often think of this as "making too much of something." Doing this prevents your body's systems from returning to a normal level and thus makes you susceptible to further aggravation and annoyance. Therefore, prolonged anger makes it easier for you to get angry the next time something goes wrong. Furthermore, prolonged anger will make your conflict that much harder (if not completely impossible) to resolve.

4. *When it leads to aggression.* Aggressive acts are sure to get you into trouble. When you feel you have been abused or treated unfairly, you may want to lash out at the person who has offended you. Anger, particularly when intense and personal, pushes for an aggressive response. Your muscles get tense, your voice gets louder and you clench your fists and stare sharply. When you are in that state, you are more likely to act on impulse. Physical aggression and verbal aggression (like calling someone a jerk) are ineffective ways of dealing with conflict. If your anger makes you aggressive, you have a problem.

5. ***When it disturbs school, work or relationships.*** When your anger makes it hard for people to relate to you, it becomes costly. Your anger will prevent you from concentrating on work or school and will keep you from being satisfied with what you do. Your anger will often repel other people and make it difficult for them to like you.

Ask yourself these five questions about your anger:
1. Is it too frequent?
   2. Is it too intense?
      3. Does it last too long?
         4. Does it lead to aggression?
            5. Does it disturb school, work or your relationships?

If you answered "Yes" to any of these questions, anger is a problem in your life. After we've worked awhile on solving this problem, I will ask you to re-take this test. If you can then answer "No" to a question to which you had previously answered "Yes," then you'll know that you've made progress.

Test #2:
How Often Do You Get Angry?
This test has two parts.

Part I
Listed next are a number of statements that people use to describe themselves. Read each statement and then indicate how often you feel this way. Do so by choosing a number from the box that best corresponds with your answer. Remember that there are no right or wrong answers to this test. Do not spend too much time on any one statement—simply give the answer which *best* seems to describe how you *generally* feel.

Fill in <u>1</u> for *Almost never*   Fill in <u>3</u> for *Often*
Fill in <u>2</u> for *Sometimes*   Fill in <u>4</u> for *Almost always*

How I Generally Feel

_____ 1. I am quick tempered.

_____ 2. I have a fiery temper.

_____ 3. I am a hotheaded person.

_____ 4. I get angry when I'm slowed down by others' mistakes.

_____ 5. I feel annoyed when people don't recognize my good work.

_____ 6. I fly off the handle.

_____ 7. When I get mad, I say nasty things.

_____ 8. It makes me furious when I am criticized in front of others.

_____ 9. When I get frustrated, I feel like hitting someone.

_____ 10. I feel infuriated when I do a good job and get a poor evaluation.

Part II

Everyone feels angry or furious from time to time, but people differ in the ways in which they react when they are angry. Listed next are a number of statements which people use to describe their reactions when they feel *angry* or *furious*. Read each statement and then fill in the line with the number which indicates how *often* you *generally* react or behave in the manner described. Remember that there are no right or wrong answers to this test. Do not spend too much time on any one statement.

Fill in <u>1</u> for *Almost never*   Fill in <u>3</u> for *Often*

Fill in <u>2</u> for *Sometimes*   Fill in <u>4</u> or *Almost always*

When Angry or Furious . . .

_____ 1. I do not control my temper.

_____ 2. I express my anger with verbal attacks.

_____ 3. I keep things in.

_____ 4. I am impatient with others.

_____ 5. I pout or sulk.

_____ 6. I withdraw from people.

_____ 7. I make sarcastic remarks to others.

_____ 8. I rarely keep my cool.

_____ 9. I do things like slam doors.

_____ 10. I boil inside, but I don't show it.

_____ 11. I can't control my behavior.

_____ 12. I argue with others.

_____ 13. I tend to harbor grudges that I don't tell anyone about.

_____ 14. I strike out at whatever infuriates me.

_____ 15. I cannot stop myself from losing my temper.

_____ 16. I am secretly quite critical of others.

_____ 17. I am angrier than I am willing to admit.

_____ 18. I calm down slower than most other people.

_____ 19. I say nasty things.

_____ 20. I try to be tolerant and understanding, but I usually fail.

_____ 21. I'm irritated a great deal more than people are aware of.

_____ 22. I lose my temper a lot.

_____ 23. If someone annoys me, I'm tell him in abusive words how I feel.

_____ 24. I have trouble controlling my angry feelings.

Now add up your scores for Part I and Part II separately. Write the totals below:
Part I _____
Part II _____

Now compare your scores to those given below:

	Part I	Part II
Male Adolescents	27	35
Female Adolescents	27	38

If your totals are equal to or greater than the numbers in the table, you probably have an anger problem. Individuals who scored highly on Part I often experience anger and feel that they are treated unfairly by others. They are likely to experience a great deal of frustration. This part of the test measures a general tendency to experience and express anger without specific provocation.

Part II of the test measures how frequently you express your anger in actions, regardless of how you try to control it. A high score here indicates that you express anger more frequently than normal. You may manifest anger in many facets of your behavior. You may have difficulty in relationships and are at risk to develop medical and psychological disorders. If you scored highly on either part of this test, then the need for you to change is serious. Reading this book may be the best thing you have ever done for yourself.

As I mentioned earlier, I will ask you to take these tests again later so that we can measure your progress. I want you to remember that you are not bad or sick or crazy because you have an anger problem. This is not a black mark on your worth as a person. Anger problems are learned and can be unlearned. For example, fifty percent of all aggressive individuals either witnessed or experienced physical abuse as they were growing up. For these individuals, acting out verbally or physically came to be seen as an acceptable method for releasing anger. Some of you may have a parent who enrages you but keeps you from expressing your anger by being punitive or abusive. If this describes your situation, then you probably over-control your anger. Some of you may have grown up in a broken family with few rules but a great deal of acting out in anger. If this describes your situation, then you probably under-control your anger. Remember that there are probably deep reasons why you express your anger the way you do—it is not a matter of your being a "bad" person.

Teen Anger Tips

- Actions committed in anger will take a toll on your relationships with others. They will also take a toll on **you**.
- Angry acts may sometimes be illegal.
- Distinguish between expressing anger in words and expressing it in actions.
- Learn to deal with your anger by first saying, "I feel angry right now because…"
- Understand that males and females are equally likely to express anger in destructive ways.
- Remember that anger has to do with exerting power and control.
- Be aware of the three ways to deal with anger: internalizing it, over-controlling it and under-controlling it.
- Use the tests I've given you to measure your progress.
- Accept that you are not bad, sick or crazy.
- Learn the reasons why you act the way you do.
- Know that if you have learned problem behaviors, you can unlearn them.

chapter 4

Teen Anger Management Workshop Model

Will I ever see the light?
Even though I'm falling.
Will there ever be any peace for me?
Even though I'm falling.
-Saliva, "Your Disease"

Remember, as I said earlier, in the many anger management classes I have conducted for teenagers over the years, most teens do not come voluntarily or willingly. Usually they were pushed to come by their parents, ordered to appear by a judge or forced to attend by their schools in lieu of a suspension. However, the good news is that many of these sessions have been very successful. I've seen remarkable turn-arounds in relatively little time. I want you to feel encouraged by this. In this chapter, we will discuss more aspects of these sessions and what you might learn from them.

Because most teens come to these classes expecting to be judged and misunderstood, they are usually very defensive. However, as each person tells the group how he or she came to be there and the group listens to each story, understanding and trust slowly build. I ask the group not to confront the speaker, only to listen. Many teenagers who are angry feel that no one ever truly listens to them. Perhaps you feel this way, too. After we've established a climate of trust and acceptance, the group is ready to learn important tips about healthy and unhealthy ways to express anger. These tips will hopefully change how you feel about handling your life.

As I mentioned, teens who attend my workshop begin by telling the group how they came to be there. In just the same way, I want you to write down how you came to be using this book. Don't worry if you feel that this book was forced upon you. You can start by writing *My therapist forced it on me* or *My parents bought it for me and said "Here, read this."* Don't stop there, though. Go on to explain *why* you think that other person wants you to read it:

Teen Anger Exercise: Why Are You Reading This Book?

_____

_____

_____

_____

_____

Did you write about a time when someone provoked you or pushed your buttons and caused you to lose control? If so, then you are not alone. Many other people have been in situations where they've felt provoked and then lost it. No doubt, you probably *were* provoked to anger. Nobody gets angry for absolutely no reason. The heat of the moment then caused you to lose your cool. You were not able to perceive the subtle buildup of feelings, sensations and behaviors which led to your eruption. You were probably more focused on what the other person was saying or doing, rather than what was going on inside of you.

One way you can help change this behavior is by thinking more positively. The teens who have attended my workshops often had many negative thoughts about themselves and about entering counseling when they begin. It is important for you to learn, as they did, to dispute those negative thoughts and replace them with positive ones. We can control what we choose to think about the world, about other people and about ourselves. For example, many teens who have come to see me resented having to come to counseling. In our sessions together, they learned to replace this negative thought with a positive one, such as: *Well, since I have to be here anyway, I might as well get something out of it.* The teens in these sessions often harbored feelings of guilt and shame. They thought they were bad, sick or crazy. How else could they explain having to see a shrink? The fact is that I work with normal, everyday people who are simply having problems in life. My patients are all contributing members of society with positive as well as negative traits. Those who seek treatment are usually overwhelmed by their problems. They are often demoralized by them. Remember: counseling is a process of remoralization. Therapy can help a person change his or her thoughts and actions to overcome problems in living. Replace your negative thoughts with positive ones such as:

I am not bad. I am not sick. I am not crazy.
I learned faulty behavior and ways of thinking and I can unlearn them.
There are reasons why I have acted as I have.
I can change.

No doubt you have had negative thoughts about yourself and your behavior, just as the teens in my counseling sessions did. In the space that follows, write down those negative thoughts. Then change each of those negative thoughts into positive ones. For example, you could change the negative thought, *I'm a bad person because I get angry all the time*, into the positive thought, *I'm not bad because I feel angry—I just need to manage my anger better*. Notice how you can choose to think differently about things and about yourself.

Negative Thought

1) _____

_____

_____

_____

2) _____

_____

_____

_____

3) _____

_____

_____

_____

4) _____

_____

_____

_____

Positive Thought

1) _____

_____

_____

_____

2) _____

_____

_____

_____

3) _____

_____

_____

_____

4) _____

_____

_____

_____

I teach teens in counseling that they should not say "I just snap," "I just go off" or "I don't know what comes over me" when they get angry. These statements imply a lack of control. If it were true that these teens could never control themselves, then they would be beyond help! It is important for teens to realize that they still retain *some* control when they get angry. When a teen tells me that he or she "just snapped," I dispute that notion by asking such questions as:

- "Did you hit the person as hard as you possibly could?"
- "Did you go off on the principal or some kid who was in the wrong place at the wrong time?"
- "Did you choose to punch, scratch or slap him or her?"
- "Did you knock your computer monitor or your boom box onto the floor?"

These questions help teens with anger problems realize that they've been making choices about how they express their anger, even though they didn't know it. An "aha" expression often comes over their faces when this realization sets in. They've learned a major lesson that anger is something they can control.

The next lesson has to do with provocation. Teens often explain their angry behavior by saying things like:

- "She made me do it."
- "He knows just how to push my buttons."
- "She dissed me in front of the other kids."
- "He got right in my face."
- "She called me out."
- "He called my girlfriend a whore."

I tell those teens that I believe these explanations—I accept that another person provoked them to anger. Teens always express relief at this. However, I quickly add that although this may have been true, it was their choice to act on that anger and express it in destructive ways. It does not matter what other people have said or done. Ultimately, an individual only has control over what he or she does. Remember, as I've told these teens, you are the only one responsible for your destructive actions, so therefore *you* must be the one to change those actions. Accepting responsibility produces a desire for change. At this point, the teens in my workshops often raise a clamor for help: "Okay, Doc, I can see what's got to be done. So now, how do I do that?"

Once teens make this realization, they see that they are empowered to change. They are no longer caught up by destructive, hurtful anger. Now that they are ready, we discuss a number of specific techniques or tools that can help. These tools will reinforce the notion that they are in control and can make choices. They can more readily accept the lessons, because these techniques give them concrete, immediate ways they can change.

In the chapters that follow, you will learn some of these specific techniques and tools to help you change your reactions when you feel provoked by others. We will look at more real-life stories about people who used these tools to change their behavior in their own lives. I ask that you complete some more short exercises and quizzes that will keep you on your toes and reinforce what you've learned. We will discuss when it is best to seek professional help and how to do it. You will learn techniques to measure your changes and reward yourself for your efforts. You will learn how to ask for feedback from others, such as parents, teachers, friends, girlfriends, boyfriends and bosses. We will bring your anger problems out into the light so you can overcome them and develop feelings of self-worth that will change your life forever.

Teen Anger Tips

- When you are provoked to feel anger, remember that nobody gets angry for no reason at all.
- Pay attention to what is going on inside of you rather than focusing on what others say or do.
- You can control what you choose to think about the world, about others and about yourself.
- Replace negative thoughts with positive ones.
- When you get angry, you are still in control.
- Although others may provoke you, it is only you who chooses to act out in anger.
- Regardless of what another person has said or done, acting out on your anger is destructive and ultimately hurts you.
- You only have control over yourself. You have no control over what other people say or do.
- It is okay to accept responsibility and acknowledge that you have choices and are in control.
- Accept change.

chapter 5

Anger Is Okay

I'm bouncing off the walls again...
Pull myself together just to fall once more.
- Sugarcult, "Bouncing Off the Walls"

It's okay for you to feel anger; what causes problems is how you choose to express that anger. Even at the moment when you are most angry, you still exercise control and make choices about how to express yourself. Here is an exercise that will reinforce this point.

Teen Anger Exercise

Write down examples of things you've done in anger. Then, across from each example, write more extreme versions of these actions.

My Angry Act
"I threw the plate at the wall."

"I cursed at her."

More Extreme Version
"I threw the plate at my brother's head and sent him to the hospital."

"I cursed her out and said that I wished she wasn't my mother."

1) _____

   _____

   _____

2) _____

   _____

   _____

1) _____

   _____

   _____

2) _____

   _____

   _____

3) _____   3) _____

_____   _____

_____   _____

4) _____   4) _____

_____   _____

_____   _____

Do you see the differences between the two columns? Do these differences show you that you are able to exercise control and make choices, even when you are angry?

Teen Anger Exercise

This exercise will help you learn that although others may provoke you to anger, no one can force you to act in a certain way. You *make a choice* when you lash out in anger. In the space that follows, you will find statements that describe actions committed in anger. The statements in the left column place responsibility for the action on another person's shoulders. The speaker claims that another person *forced* him/her to act in this way. The statements in the right column show you how to accept responsibility for the action. The speaker admits that he/she *chose* to act in that manner. Read these examples and note the difference between the two columns:

"Forced" Action

"She made me angry, so I *had* to slap her."

"He dissed me in front of the other kids, so I *was forced* to yell at him."

Chosen Action

"She made me angry, so I *chose* to slap her."

"He dissed me in front of the other kids, so I *decided* to yell at him."

Now read the statements in the left column below. Note how the speaker claims to have been forced to act in a certain way. Rewrite these statements so that they now reflect a choice. Use words such as "I chose" or "I decided."

"Forced" Action

1) "My friend embarrassed me in public, so I was forced to hit him."

Chosen Action

_____

_____

_____

2) "The teacher criticized me
and got me so angry that I had
to throw my books on the floor." _____

3) "She made me look like a
fool, so I had no other choice
but to blow my top." _____

In the space that follows, write down statements you've used to explain how you were "forced" to act in anger. Now change those statements so that they reflect choices:

1) _____   1) _____

2) _____   2) _____

3) _____   3) _____

The purpose of this exercise is to help you learn that you are in control and responsible for your behavior. This knowledge will empower you to feel that you are not helpless in the face of your problem. You are in charge. Here is a story about one of my former patients that will reinforce this point.

The Mountain Man

When Jerry first met with me, I saw a big, burly nineteen-year-old college freshman. He used fake identification to get into bars where he drank heavily and got into fistfights with other patrons. Eventually, he was kicked out of school, the police locked him up for fighting and a judge ordered him to attend my workshop.

My first impression of him was that he would be a tough case, because he had been ordered to come against his will and because he seemed accustomed to always having things his way. The group felt intimidated by him. In truth, it turned out that he was more intimidated by us. Jerry turned out to be a gentle giant. He opened up slowly and revealed himself to be intelligent and articulate. He did well in the group, made good contributions and eventually graduated from the program. He had stopped his violent behavior.

A few years later, I found myself working late when the phone rang. When I answered, I heard Jerry's voice. He was calling from another state where he had moved with his girlfriend. He reported that since the end of our sessions, he had not been arrested, nor had he gotten into any bar fights, nor had he abused his girlfriend. In fact, he had returned to college part-time and hoped to receive his degree in a year. Also, he and his girlfriend had gotten engaged and were planning to marry. Jerry thanked me. He said his father had raised him to believe that a man should never express his feelings. Our group workshop had been the first time he had ever opened up about himself. He learned that it was okay to have emotions and to share them. Jerry learned that he could be accepted by others and that he could accept himself. The six-week program had changed his life and he had just wanted to let me know that. I was deeply moved by this call. After twenty-one years in practice, this simple "thank you" stands out as my fondest memory. It makes me feel so good to help a person change. I want this book to help you in just the same way.

I hope Jerry's story gives you great hope and makes you eager to continue. The process is not easy, but remember that I'll be there to cheer you on. Just like the teens in my workshops, you may feel in the beginning as though you've been forced into this process, but you'll soon grow to appreciate it. You may have been put off at first, but soon you'll be adopting the tools and skills in this book as your own. Like the teens I have counseled, I hope you are thinking, "Okay, Doc, I can see that I have a problem. So what do I do about it?" The rest of this book will answer that question.

Teen Anger Tips

- ◆ It's okay to feel anger; what causes problems is how we choose to express that anger.
- ◆ Even when you are at your angriest, you still make choices about how to act.
- ◆ Other people cannot force you to act a certain way. Take responsibility for yourself and admit that you *choose* how you act.
- ◆ You are not helpless; you are in charge.
- ◆ Look at this process of making change within yourself as an adventure.
- ◆ Remember, I am your ally in this process.

part III

Teen Anger Insights

chapter 6

You Make My Head Feel Like It's Going to Explode: Early Warning Signs

*My mind's broken, I'm goin up in smoke
if you breathe my toke I'm guaranteeing you choke...*
- Saliva, "Your Disease"

Many teens tell me that when they get angry, they just "go off" and explode without warning. This is something I've heard repeated many times. Sometimes teens feel this excuses their behavior and lets them avoid taking responsibility for their actions. What they really seem to be saying is: *How can you blame me for what I do if I can't control myself?* But if this excuse were completely true, then there would be no hope for change. As has been explained earlier, if one is never in control, one can never gain control. In order to change, teens must first understand that they still are in control even when they are angry. Once they realize this, they must learn to increase their level of control before anger sweeps them away. Teens can do this by staying alert to early warning signs that signal an anger attack. Identifying these signs will help you get hold of your anger early on, long before it becomes explosive.

There are a great many signs that may precede an anger attack, such as muscle tension, knots in the stomach, clenched fists, teeth-grinding or a pounding heart. When I get angry, I can feel my face flush. I can literally feel the heat spreading into my face. Remember, no one just "explodes" in anger without warning signs. In this chapter, we will review the most common warning signs described earlier and discuss ways you can recognize them before you get angry.

There are many different cues that accompany the emotion of anger. As we discussed in chapter 2, we can sort these signs into three broad groups: sensations, actions and thoughts. Let's review these groups again, one by one.

Here are some **sensations** you might be feeling right before you get angry:

- Feeling your face flush
- Blood rushing through your veins
- Heart pounding
- Breathing becomes faster, unsteady or shallow
- Feeling hot or feeling cold
- Feeling pain in your neck (hence the expression "pain in the neck")

Here are some **actions** you might unconsciously be performing right before the onset of anger:

- Clenching your fists
- Clenching your jaw
- Grinding your teeth
- Tensing and flexing your muscles
- Pacing around the room
- Inability to sit or stand still

Here are some **thoughts** that might signal an anger attack:

- *He did this to me out of spite.*
- *She did this to me purposely.*
- *I can't believe he did that.*
- *No one talks to me like that.*
- *I'll show her.*
- *Now everyone is laughing at me.*

Be careful when taking note of the thoughts that signal an anger attack. Oftentimes, thinking about what has made us angry only makes us angrier. These thoughts fuel the anger and the anger then fuels the thoughts, thus trapping us in a vicious cycle. I will return to this subject later in the book.

Exercise

Write down the sensations, actions and thoughts that you usually experience right *before* you get angry.

Sensations

_____

_____

_____

_____

Actions

_____

_____

_____

_____

Thoughts

_____

_____

_____

_____

Try to remember your early warning signals. The earlier you can recognize them, the better you will be able to deal with your anger and express it properly. You will be less caught up by anger and more in control of the situation.

Whenever we talk about a conflict, we can always find something that has provoked the conflict in the first place. I use the word "trigger" to describe the thing that originally provoked the conflict. There are many different kinds of triggers.

Sometimes a trigger may be something that someone has said:
- Someone tells you what to do.
- Someone calls you a name.

Or it may be an action that someone does:
- Someone pushes or hits you.
- Someone makes an obscene gesture.

In each of these cases, the trigger exists outside of us, so I call them "external triggers." Try to think about some external triggers that have provoked you to anger recently. Was it something that someone said to you? Was it something that someone did? Write down as many as you can think of.

_____

_____

_____

_____

_____

_____

_____

_____

Most of the time, it will take more than just an external trigger to get you angry. External triggers will provoke thoughts and reactions in your mind. Often, it will be these thoughts that ultimately determine whether or not you become angry. An external trigger might lead you to think things like:

- *That S.O.B. is making fun of me.*
- *She has no right to tell me what to do.*
- *I'm going to have to punch him for what he said about my friend.*
- *No one gets away with that.*

These thoughts may lead you to become angry, so they are also triggers to anger. Because they occur inside of us, I like to call them "internal triggers." You can't control external triggers, but you can control internal triggers. When you have an angry thought, you can learn how to express and deal with it properly. In the chapters that follow, you will learn how.

I once had an English teacher in high school whose anger was triggered when the class talked and didn't pay attention to him. His anger would build up—we could tell because his face turned red. He would then start pacing back and forth with the chalk in his hands as he lectured and wrote on the blackboard. If he heard someone talking, he would spin around to glare at the class and then spin back to the chalkboard. People continued talking and his spins became 360-degree turns. At this point we always started laughing. Then he turned around and called us "big mouths" or "suburban snobs." We laughed more. One time he actually stood up on top of a three-foot bookshelf and swung the emergency fire window wide open. He yelled "I'm going to jump, I'm going to jump!" He was not kidding. He was in a genuine rage. The tension broke when one of my classmates hollered back, "Jump!" Everyone, including the teacher, started laughing. Talk about being embarrassed. You might imagine how you look to others when you act on your anger quickly and without control, as this man did.

My teacher was not particularly effective in managing classroom behavior. He blew up and then calmed down. He never did anything to change the way we acted. We talked in class because we knew nothing would happen to us. On the other hand, I once had a social studies teacher who took over the classroom in a split-second. On the first day of class, the bell rang and we all continued talking as we slowly took our seats. No one paid attention to the new teacher who stood at the front of the room with his arms folded. We kept on talking. All of a sudden we heard an explosion and jumped out of our seats. The teacher had been standing behind a metal garbage can next to his desk—I suppose he had been quietly positioning it. He had kicked the garbage can straight down the middle row, at ear-level. It had hit the cinder block wall at the back of the room with a metallic blast. We silently stared at the teacher as he slowly walked down the middle aisle, picking up scattered pieces of trash and putting them back in the can.

The teacher explained that no one had been in any danger. He said he was a black belt in Tae Kwon Do and knew exactly where the can was going. The teacher explained that he intended never to wait for us again. From then on, he demanded that we enter class on time and sit silently until he was ready to start. He said he would give us a demonstration of Tae Kwon Do at the end of the quarter. The teacher also told us that, if there was enough interest, he would start coaching students in martial arts after school. Sure enough, he started a martial arts club and this new teacher soon became very popular. Although his action appeared aggressive, the teacher had complete control of the flight of the garbage can. He had gotten our attention and had very calmly explained what he wanted from us. His outburst was effective and caused us to respect him. That is what his martial arts training had taught. Many of you are probably aware that those so trained do not use their skills to act aggressively but only to defend themselves. The martial arts teach self-control and discipline. You might consider taking this kind of training in addition to reading this book.

Teen Anger Exercise
List Your Common Triggers:

External:

_____

_____

_____

_____

_____

_____

Internal:

_____

_____

_____

_____

_____

When you become aware of the triggers that are most likely to set you off, you will be better prepared to head off an anger attack before it erupts. You will be able to say to yourself, "Okay, this situation is familiar. It has triggered anger before. I know I need to deal with it differently." We will discuss *how* to deal with your anger later in the book. For now, simply note that you have become more aware of *when* you are about to get angry. You are already becoming your own teacher and therapist!

Teen Anger Exercise: Journaling

The pages that follow will provide a space for you to write down what you feel when you get angry. Before you write on these pages, make several photocopies of them so that you can use the Anger Journal again and again.

Keeping this journal will help you change how you deal with your anger. When you write down how you feel, you will release your anger rather than keeping it in or acting on it. If you can't complete a journal entry in the heat of the moment (because you are too emotional) wait a little while and complete it some time afterward. Writing these entries will help you learn a great deal about your anger. Look for repeating patterns: Are there common triggers which always set you off? Do you always deal with your anger in a consistent way? Does your behavior have common consequences? The information you learn from this journal will help you recognize and change old patterns of behavior.

Teen Anger Journal

Date:_____

Intensity: Circle the number that best expresses how angry you are. The scale starts at the number one (the least angry) and goes up to number ten (the most angry).

1. Irritated
2. Frustrated
3. Annoyed
4. Angry
5. Mad
6. Pissed
7. Enraged
8. Furious
9. Explosive
10. Physically and/or verbally aggressive

Anger Cues

What physical sensations, if any, did you experience in the moments just before you felt angry?

_____

_____

_____

Were you acting in a particular way in the moments just before you felt angry?

_____

_____

_____

What thoughts were you thinking in the moments just before you felt angry?

_____

_____

_____

Triggers

What caused you to feel angry? What were the external triggers? The internal triggers?

_____

_____

_____

How did you express you anger? What did you do? How did you act?

_____

_____

_____

What happened after you expressed your anger? What consequences followed as a result of your behavior?

_____

_____

_____

Were you under the influence of alcohol or drugs? Yes _____ No _____

Teen Anger Tips

- ◆ No one "explodes" from anger without warning. Learn to identify the cues that signal you are about to get angry.
- ◆ The cues that signal anger may be sensations, actions or thoughts.
- ◆ Watch out when taking note of your angry thoughts. Those thoughts can fuel angry feelings, which can then fuel angry thoughts, and so on, in a dangerous cycle.
- ◆ The earlier you recognize you are angry, the better your chances to control what you do with your anger.
- ◆ Everyone has his or her own triggers that typically provoke anger.
- ◆ Triggers can be both internal and external.
- ◆ When you become aware of your most common triggers, you will be on guard before anger can get the best of you.
- ◆ When provoked by a common trigger, learn to say: "Okay, this situation is familiar. It's triggered anger before. I know I need to deal with it differently."
- ◆ Use the Anger Journal to explore your feelings and learn about your anger.
- ◆ Writing in a journal is a constructive way of expressing your anger.

chapter 7

Losing the Battle but Winning the War: It's Okay to Walk Away

Today, I changed…I'm gone, so long
Break out, 'cause I'm better off on my own.
- Sugarcult, "Stuck In America"

Although the concept of taking a "Time Out" was introduced in chapter 2, here we will explore it in more depth. Perhaps when you were a small child, your parents punished you by giving you a Time Out. If so, you may now laugh at the idea of using a Time Out to manage your anger. Don't be put off, though. The Time Out we will use is not a child's punishment, nor is it something your parents will make you do. It is something you will choose to do yourself. As explained briefly in chapter 2, the Time Out is an excellent anger management tool. If you notice you are experiencing any early warning signs of anger (sensations, actions or thoughts) or if you are provoked by any anger triggers, taking a Time Out will help you chill out. It is your responsibility to call a Time Out for yourself—no one else's. Remember, when you do call a Time Out, stay away from the anger-triggering situation or person for as long as it takes you to cool down. Spend that time trying to relax. Engage in an activity that you find calming or tension-easing, such as walking, running, playing sports, listening to music, calling a friend, taking a bath, practicing meditation, roller-blading, skate boarding or biking. The following exercise will help you recognize activities that relax you and provide you with the opportunity to plan ahead for your Time Out.

Teen Anger Relaxation Exercise

What activities do you find relaxing? Write them down here.

_____
_____
_____
_____
_____

It's a good idea to plan a Time Out before you need it. In the space which follows, write down some ways you will relax yourself during your next Time Out.

_____
_____
_____
_____
_____

Remember, during your Time Out, do not engage in aggressive activities like hitting a punching bag or driving fast. These activities merely sustain your angry feelings. Do not use alcohol or drugs during a Time Out. Again, allow your Time Out to last a few minutes or a few hours, but don't let it stretch beyond that. After you have cooled down, return to the situation that provoked the angry feelings. If you don't do this, the other people involved might think you have "blown them off." If you feel angry again after you've returned, call for a second Time Out. Take as many Time Outs as you need.

If you haven't already, explain the concept of the Time Out to your family and friends. If you already have, make them aware you are still using the Time Out technique to deal with your anger. In this way, they will be cooperative when you take a Time Out. Remind them that only you can call your own Time Out and only you can end it. Make sure they understand that they must not try to stop you from leaving the room, nor should they follow you out. Let all discussion stop. Do not call a Time Out in a hostile way. Don't shout it, don't sneak in some angry last words and don't slam the door on your way out. Make sure all your family members have read this chapter and thoroughly understand the ground rules for a Time Out.

Time Outs must give you the chance to get away from upsetting thoughts which prolong anger. Distract yourself from any thoughts related to the situation. You may have to do this several times, since angry thoughts will tend to creep back in. We will revisit this subject again in a later chapter. Return to the situation only when you think you can talk about your anger calmly. If you need to, take another Time Out.

Time Out Exercise

Write a script for how you will implement a Time Out. What will you say? What will you do? How will you return to the situation? How will you react if the other person doesn't cooperate with the Time Out?

Now that you've written down a Time Out, ask a family member or friend to rehearse it with you. This will be a sort of "dry run." Practice calling the Time Out, engaging in a relaxing activity and then joining up again with the other person. By practicing the Time Out when you are still calm, you will know exactly what to do when you get angry.

Teen Anger Exercise

Having practiced your Time Out, write a review of how it went. What happened? What did you say? What did the other person say? Did you feel your dry-run was successful? What do you need to work on? Ask the other person for feedback and write his or her comments down as well. Practice your Time Out again after making any necessary changes.

There will be times when it won't be appropriate for you to take a formal Time Out, such as when you are at school or work. In these situations, call the Time Out to yourself and engage in an appropriate relaxing activity.

When you are at school, you can try sitting at your desk and relax, using the techniques outlined in chapter 2. But don't fall asleep! I'll have more to say on this subject in the next chapter.

If you call a Time Out while you are driving in a car, have everyone stop discussion. Relax. Distract yourself from thoughts related to the anger. You might consider turning on the radio, as long as this doesn't lead to a fight over which station to play. Resume conversation only when you feel calm enough to talk again.

If you learn to call a Time Out each and every time you notice anger signs and triggers, you will never again express your anger in a destructive way. Do not deviate from this procedure! The Time Out will always work, as long as you use it consistently and correctly. Don't use the Time Out for a few days and then drop it—*keep on using it*. I have seen this too many times in my practice: teens will avoid a few arguments using the Time Out and then forget about it altogether, because it seems easier to drop it. Don't be this way! Change is going to take hard work, so stick to the use of Time Outs consistently. Use them *every time* you are in an argument and get angry.

Some of you may have attitudes that make it hard for you to call a Time Out. Our society teaches us to never walk away from a fight. Some people see "walking away" as a weakness, but they are wrong. It takes great strength to call a Time Out and walk away. It's definitely harder and takes more courage to exert self-control than it is to submit to the false bravado of lashing out in anger. Later on in this book, I'll talk more about this subject in relation to peer pressure.

Teen Anger Exercise

What makes it hard for you to walk away from an argument? Write these things down in the space provided. Across from each entry, explain why it is better for you to take a Time Out and walk away.

WHY IT'S HARD TO WALK AWAY
"If I don't stand up to him, he'll think I'm chicken."

WHY IT'S BETTER TO TAKE A TIME OUT
"I will stand up to him, but only calmly. Getting angry won't help."

1) _____

1) _____

2) _____
_____
_____

2) _____
_____
_____

3) _____
_____
_____

3) _____
_____
_____

4) _____
_____
_____

4) _____
_____
_____

Teen Time Out Tips

- Time Outs are not meant as punishments. Use them as anger management tools.
- Call a Time Out whenever you notice your common cues and triggers to anger.
- It is your responsibility to call a Time Out for yourself.
- Leave without anger and relax. Do not stew and brew.
- Return to the situation as soon as you can. Don't wait more than a couple of hours.
- After your anger has cooled, check in with the other person and try to work things out.
- Explain the Time Out to others ahead of time while you are still calm. Don't wait to explain it during an argument.
- You may take more than one Time Out.
- Practice a "dry-run" of your Time Out.
- Adapt the Time Out to fit other situations (such as school or work) when it would be inappropriate for you to leave the room.
- If you call a Time Out while driving in a car, have everyone stop all discussion.
- So long as you use the Time Out consistently and correctly, you will never act out in anger again.
- Walking away makes you strong, not weak.

chapter 8

Mellowing Out: If You're Cool, You Can't Be Angry

> *I wonder what it takes to make this*
> *one better place, let's erase the wasted*
> *Take the evil out the people they'll be acting right...*
> - Tupac Shakur, "Changes"

Now that you have learned to identify the warning signs and triggers that lead to your anger, here are some excellent techniques to help you lessen that anger. I call these "anger reducers." Learning these anger reducers will help you to have greater self-control so you will be able to deal with your angry feelings more effectively. Remember: you *must* start an anger reducer the very moment you notice one of your anger cues or triggers. Don't wait and don't forget. When you notice that you are experiencing a sign or trigger to anger, use one of these exercises.

Anger Reducers

1. **Deep breathing.** Slow yourself down by taking long, deep breaths. Doing this will give you more control in a pressure situation. This exercise is much like taking a few deep breaths before shooting a free throw in basketball. Deep breathing will relieve your tension and put you at ease.

2. **Counting backward.** Silently count backward at an even pace from twenty to one. This exercise will give you more control and allow you time to think about how to respond to the situation.

3. **Imagining pleasant thoughts.** Imagine yourself in a peaceful
    place (you may remember I first introduced this technique in
    chapter 1). Use your imagination to transport yourself to this
    calm, restful place. Doing this will relax your body and calm your
    mind.

Remember that relaxation and anger are opposing forces—one can-
cels out the other. You cannot be relaxed and angry at the same time, so
use relaxation to dispel your anger. Research has shown that people can
develop extraordinary control over their bodies through such activities as
meditation, self-hypnosis, biofeedback and relaxation training. These
techniques increase the occurrence of something called "Alpha waves" in
the brain. These Alpha waves are associated with states of deep relaxation. The bottom line is that you can train your body to relax and thus
reduce your anger. Training yourself to relax on cue is not as hard as you
might think. In the pages that follow, you will learn more exercises that
will help you develop this skill.

Our minds are complicated things. Psychologists have found that
what we feel, what we think and what we do influence one other in complicated ways. No doubt you've heard the old riddle, "What came first,
the chicken or the egg?" Well, psychologists wonder a similar thing
about us: which comes first, our emotions, our thoughts or our actions?
It's not an easy question to answer. The important thing to know is that
this cycle of feeling, thinking and acting drives and reinforces itself. To
help you understand this better, think back to the last time you felt angry.
At some point, you probably stopped to think about what had made you
angry. When you thought about this, you became even angrier. When
you became angrier, you acted out destructively. Thus your feelings
influenced your thoughts, your thoughts in turn influenced your feelings
and your feelings influenced your behavior.

We can take this one step farther. When you acted destructively, you
dispelled some of your anger. When you dispelled some of your anger,
you felt relief. When you felt relief, you learned to repeat your behavior
the next time you got angry. Thus your behavior influenced your future
thoughts. Do you see how the cycle works? Your thoughts influenced
your feelings and your feelings influenced your actions. Your actions then
let you release your anger and feel relief, which taught you to repeat your
behavior in the future, despite the destructive consequences.

You can break this self-destructive cycle. Although it's almost impossible to control how you feel, you can learn to control what you think and

how you act. Later on in the book, you will learn ways to change your thoughts. For now, let's focus on changing how you act. Relaxation will be the key to helping you change your destructive behavior.

In the pages that follow, I will introduce a formal relaxation method that will help you curb your anger. I will guide you step by step, giving you exercises to practice these techniques. This practice will help you become better and better at relaxing. In fact, anyone can benefit from practicing these relaxation techniques once a day or whenever stress accumulates. These techniques can also help you fall asleep whenever you have trouble sleeping. You can start your relaxation by saying to yourself, "I will relax just for the sake of relaxing," or you can say, "I will relax for the purpose of falling asleep." State your purpose before you begin, so that you are clear about what you expect to achieve.

When I teach my patients this technique, I usually make them an audiotape that walks them through the entire exercise. I tell them to use the tape at home to assist them in their practice. For the first few days, the tape helps them focus. Later on, the technique becomes second nature and the tape is no longer necessary. Although you can learn the technique without a tape, you might find a tape helpful when you first start out. You can find these kinds of relaxation tapes in many libraries and bookstores. Try to find one that gives instruction, rather than one that just plays relaxing sounds like waves or rain or music. You might also consider using subliminal tapes which involve inaudible suggestions to relax. The best tape is one that runs you through an actual relaxation technique.

If you can't find a tape that you like, make one for yourself. Take the exercises that follow and read them into a tape recorder. If you don't like listening to the sound of your own voice, have a friend make the tape for you. The person that reads the instruction should speak slowly and in a soft, soothing voice. If you prefer different parts of the exercise to others, have your tape emphasize the parts you like. Feel free to tailor the exercise to fit your individual needs. Remember that you should only use the tape until you are able to remember the exercise on your own. You should be able to throw away the tape after about three weeks of practice.

At the very beginning of this book, I introduced the phrase "Dr. Ah" to help you remember the four steps to anger management. The "A" of "Dr. Ah" stood for "Activate the relaxation response." As you may remember, I gave you a number of quick relaxation techniques in that chapter. Now I will give you a longer and more extensive relaxation technique. This technique has three phases. The first phase requires you to focus on and dissolve all the tension in the different muscles of your body.

The second phase asks you to use all of your senses to imagine yourself in a relaxing place. The third phase asks you to count backward from ten to zero while coaxing your body to relax as each number passes by.

When you first start using this technique, you should complete all three phases. After a week of practice, you can drop Phase I. After two weeks, you can drop Phase II. After three weeks, you'll be able to relax yourself on cue, just by breathing slowly and letting all your tension drain away. With only three weeks practice, you'll be able to relax your body in only a few seconds. That's a worthy goal to aim for, isn't it?

Relaxation Training

Always practice this technique in a quiet place with the lights turned down low. Make sure that you will not be interrupted—you might want to do it before your parents get home from work and when your brothers and sisters are out. Turn off the television, stereo, video game system, pager and any other device that might distract you. Don't answer the phone if it rings—let the answering machine pick up the call.

To complete this exercise, you must either lie down or sit in a comfortable chair. Whichever position you choose, try to use as few muscles as possible to hold yourself in that position. Keep your eyes open or closed, whichever you prefer. If your eyes are opened, try to keep them fixed on a single point. If your eyes begin to feel tired after awhile, it's okay to close them.

Now that you are ready, let's begin Phase I. For the moment, let whatever thoughts enter your mind come and go without trying to direct them. Don't focus on anything in particular. Just relax. Locate the muscles in your body that are relaxed and compare them to the muscles that are tense. Feel the difference between them. Now direct your attention to the muscles of your face, head and throat. Notice whether or not you feel tension in those muscles; if so, relax the tension away. Melt it away. Imagine the tension draining out of your head and pouring out of the tip of your chin. Let the tension ebb from your face. Keep your breathing even. Notice the difference between feeling tense and feeling relaxed.

Now direct your attention to the muscles in the back of your neck. This is a place where we retain a lot of tension. Notice whether or not you feel any tension in these muscles. As before, relax the tension away. Just let the tension drain out of your neck muscles. If you are lying down flat, imagine that the pillow or cushion beneath your head is a large sponge that is soaking the tension out of your neck. Notice the difference between feeling tense and feeling relaxed.

Now focus your attention on your right shoulder. This is another place where we retain a lot of tension. Notice whether or not you feel any tension in your right shoulder muscles. Move your shoulder around a little to let the tension go. Let the tension flow out of your right shoulder. Imagine the tension draining down through your right arm. Let the tension drain down through your biceps, past your elbow, through your lower arm, past your wrist, through your hand and finally out through the tips of your fingers. Notice the feeling of relaxation in your right arm. Keep your breathing even. Let yourself feel calm, peaceful and relaxed.

Now move on to your left shoulder. Notice whether or not you feel any tension in your left shoulder muscles. Let the tension drain down your left arm and out of the tips of your fingers. Enjoy feeling relaxed.

Now become aware of the rhythm of your breathing. Take notice of the air as it comes in and goes out. Don't try to control your breathing; just breathe naturally. Nice and even. Realize that breathing is an automatic reflex—you do not even have to think about breathing to do it. It is a natural body process. Let the fresh air clean the toxins out of your lungs. Feel the air as it passes through your nostrils and travels all the way down to the pit of your stomach. As you breathe out, imagine that all your tension is blowing out of your body. Every outward breath should release more and more tension from your body. With each breath, you are becoming more and more relaxed. Feel your chest rising and falling with the rhythm of your breathing. Notice any tension in the muscles of your chest. Allow your breathing to melt the tension away. Use your breath to relax the tension out of your chest muscles. As before, keep your breathing even. Maintain your calm and peaceful state.

Now focus your attention on the muscles of your stomach. Take notice of any tension there and drain it away. Relax the tension away. Blow the tension out of your body as you exhale. Let yourself relax as you inhale. You might consider saying "calm" with each inward breath and "peace" with each outward breath. Calm... Peace... Calm... Peace... in rhythm with your breathing. Repeating these words will deepen your sense of relaxation. Allow whatever thoughts come to mind to enter and leave; don't focus on any one thought in particular. Only focus on the relaxation exercise, the rhythm of your breathing and the words "calm" and "peace" as you breathe in and out. Calm... Peace... Calm... Peace... Calm... Peace...

Now focus your attention on the muscles in your upper back. If you feel any tension there, take notice of it and then drain it away. If you are lying down, imagine that the surface beneath you is a big sponge soaking the tension out of the muscles of your upper back. Now move on to your lower back. This is yet another place where we retain a lot of tension. Take notice of any tension here and melt it away. Drain it away with the rhythm of your breathing. Notice the difference between feeling tense and feeling relaxed. Give special attention to this area if you have back problems. As you breathe out, imagine that you are blowing out the tension from the muscles of your lower back. Relax those muscles more and more with each outward breath. Feel calm and peaceful, quiet and relaxed.

Now review all of the muscle groups you've covered so far. If any tension has crept back into the muscles of your head, face, neck, shoulders, arms, hands, fingers, chest, stomach, upper and lower back, direct your attention to it and relax it away. Move those muscles slightly to relax them. Take notice of the tension and drain it away. Blow it out of your body with each outward breath. Feel more and more deeply relaxed with each exhalation.

Now direct your attention to the muscles of your right buttock and the upper thigh of your right leg. Let the tension in these spots drain down and out your right leg. Imagine the tension draining down through your leg, past your knee, through your calf, past your ankle, through your foot and finally out of the tips of your toes. Notice the difference between feeling tense and feeling relaxed.

Now move on to your left buttock and the upper thigh of your left leg. Take notice of any tension there and drain it away. As you did on your right side, imagine your tension flowing down your leg and out your toes. Keep your breathing even and maintain your peaceful state.

By now, the muscles of your body should be as relaxed as they can be. If your body still feels tense somewhere, take notice of the tension and relax it away. You may feel warm or cool, heavy or light. You may feel tingly. Whatever you may feel, simply allow it to be. Don't focus your thoughts on anything in particular. From the top of your head to the tips of your toes, your body should be completely relaxed. Notice how much better you feel now, as opposed to how you felt at the beginning of the exercise. Notice the tremendous difference between feeling tense and feeling relaxed. This ends Phase I of our exercise.

Now let's move on to Phase II. Use your imagination to picture yourself in a peaceful place. For example, you might imagine yourself lying on a soft blanket in the middle of a grassy field in the country. Imagine you can feel the blanket under you as it cradles your body. Imagine you can feel the warm sun on your skin and a soft breeze blowing over you. Look up to see the blue sky and some white, puffy clouds. See the birds circling overhead. Look off in the distance to see trees swaying in the breeze at the field's edge. Take in the brilliant green of the grass and the bright yellow and white of the occasional wildflower. Listen to the breeze gently rustling the leaves of the trees. Look and see a small brook somewhere in the distance. Listen to the clear water as it tumbles over the rocks. Listen to the sound of the birds singing and the insects chirping. Smell the country air all around you. Imagine the air is so fresh that you can taste it. Keep this place fixed in your imagination and return to it whenever you need to and whenever you want to. The more you practice this exercise, the easier it will be for you to slip into this relaxing place. This ends Phase II of our exercise.

Stay in your relaxing place as we move on to Phase III. Slowly count backward from ten to zero. As each number passes by, you will feel more and more relaxed.

Ten. If you notice any tension in any muscle of your body, relax it away. Imagine that the tension simply blows out of your body with every exhalation.

Nine. Notice your breath as it comes in and goes out. Feel the air pass through your nostrils and travel all the way down to your diaphragm. With each outward breath, you should feel more and more relaxed. Feel more and more at peace.

Eight. Breathe in, saying "Calm." As you breathe out, say "Peace." Calm... Peace... Calm... Peace... Calm... Peace...

Seven. Stay in your peaceful place. Feel the warm sun on your skin and the cool breeze blowing over you.

Six. See the blue sky and the white, puffy clouds. Watch the birds as they circle overhead.

Five. Hear the sound of the leaves rustling gently in the cool breeze. Listen to the water tumbling over the rocks.

Four. Smell the fresh country air all around you. With each outward breath, become more and more relaxed. Use all your senses to create this peaceful place in your imagination.

Three. Melt away any tension left in your body with the rhythm of your breathing. Let the tension drain out of your body into the ground beneath you. Imagine that the surface beneath you is a huge sponge that sucks up any tension in your muscles.

Two. You are feeling very relaxed now. Enjoy these relaxed feelings. Keep your breathing even. Feel calm and peaceful, quiet and relaxed.

One. Now you are as relaxed as you can be. Realize that you can return to this relaxed state whenever you need or want to. The more you practice this exercise, the easier it will be for you to slip into this state of deep relaxation. Look inside yourself and find the motivation to change. Realize that you can become the person you want to be. You can achieve your goals. You can let go of tension and anger. You can express yourself calmly. Feel good about how you think, feel and behave. Feel good about yourself. Accept yourself.

We are almost finished now. When we reach zero, you may drift off to sleep, if you so choose. If not, you will emerge from the exercise feeling relaxed and refreshed. Carry with you whatever you've experienced during this relaxation exercise. Keep your breathing even. Feel the air as it comes in and goes out. With each breath, feel the energy pulsing in your body. Become more aware of your surroundings. Here it comes...

Zero.

This is the end of the exercise. Remember, you should practice the exercise either once a day or every other day. After a week's practice, you can eliminate Phase I. After two weeks, eliminate Phase II. Then you will only be doing Phase III, which incorporates all of the elements of the previous two phases. Your practice should bring you to a point where you will only need the countdown in order to relax. Soon you will become so skilled at this exercise that you will be able to relax your body on cue in a few seconds.

As you practice, feel free to replace the scene suggested in the exercise with one of your own. You might place yourself on the beach or in a hammock swinging between two trees. One of my patients would return to her childhood bedroom at her grandparents' house. She would imagine herself lying in her old bed, experiencing all of the sensations, sights, sounds, smells and tastes of that safe room. You may want to use one of your own childhood memories in a similar way. The exercise that follows will help you recall some of those memories.

Teen Anger Exercise

In the space that follows, describe two of the most relaxing places that you've ever visited in your life. Try to picture places where you felt safe, where you felt that you could let yourself go.

Imagine that you are now in the first place you've remembered.

Where are you? _____

What sensations do you feel? _____

What do you see around you? _____

What do you hear? _____

What do you smell? _____

What can you taste?_____

Now imagine that you are in the second place that you've remembered.

Where are you? _____

What sensations do you feel? _____

What do you see around you? _____

What do you hear? _____

What do you smell? _____

What can you taste?_____

Teen Anger Rating Scale

Make photocopies of this log so that you can continue to use it after all the entries are filled. Each time you practice the relaxation exercise, rate your tension before you start and rate it again after you've finished. Before you start the relaxation exercise, write down the date and then rate your tension on a scale of one to five. Let '5' stand for a state of extreme tension and '1' stand for no tension. After you've completed the exercise, rate your tension a second time. Compare the two scores.

Date	Tension Before Relaxation	Tension After Relaxation
_____	1 2 3 4 5	1 2 3 4 5
_____	1 2 3 4 5	1 2 3 4 5
_____	1 2 3 4 5	1 2 3 4 5
_____	1 2 3 4 5	1 2 3 4 5
_____	1 2 3 4 5	1 2 3 4 5
_____	1 2 3 4 5	1 2 3 4 5
_____	1 2 3 4 5	1 2 3 4 5

_____	1 2 3 4 5	1 2 3 4 5
_____	1 2 3 4 5	1 2 3 4 5
_____	1 2 3 4 5	1 2 3 4 5
_____	1 2 3 4 5	1 2 3 4 5
_____	1 2 3 4 5	1 2 3 4 5
_____	1 2 3 4 5	1 2 3 4 5

By keeping this log, you can keep track of the effect of relaxation. You will have more faith in the exercise if you continually see your ratings drop from 5 or 4 before the exercise to 2 or 1 after.

Before ending this chapter, I want to give you a variation on Phase I of the relaxation exercise. The one we just used is called "Progressive Muscle Relaxation." However, there is also another technique for Phase I called "Jacobsonian Relaxation" (named for the man who developed it). This variation will appeal to those of you who want to be a little more active. This alternate method will help you stay focused because it will give you more to do. However, if you have any orthopedic or muscle problems, you should check with your doctor before using it. Your doctor may have to modify the exercise so that you do not strain or injure that part of your body.

Phase I Variation

Take off your shoes, remove your glasses (if you wear them) and get into a comfortable position in bed or in a chair. As before, this variation will take you through each of the major muscle groups of the body. However, this time you will tense each muscle for a five-count and then relax it for a ten-count. Start with the muscles of your head and face. Knit your brow, squeeze your eyes tight, wriggle up your nose and tense your mouth and cheeks. Hold it and count to five. Feel the muscles tightening. Notice the tension building. Tighten it. Hold it. Now relax and slowly count to ten. Feel the tension draining out of the muscles. Just let it go. Notice the difference between feeling tense and feeling relaxed.

Now move on to the muscles of the back of your neck. If you are lying down, push back against the cushion or pillow beneath your head. Compress your neck muscles. Feel the tension building. Hold it for five seconds. Now relax. Slowly count to ten. Feel the tension draining. Enjoy the good feeling of relaxation.

Now move on to the muscles of your shoulders and upper back. Hunch up your shoulders. Tighten the muscles. Feel the tension building. Tighten it. Hold it for five seconds. Now relax. Let the tension drain out of your shoulders and upper back muscles. Feel the tension drain away. Notice how your muscles feel as they relax. Notice the difference between feeling tense and feeling relaxed. Let a ten-count pass before you move on.

Now focus on your lower back. Arch your back and tighten those muscles. Let the tension build. Hold it for five seconds. Now relax. Just let the tension drain away. Feel the tension leave you. Enjoy the relaxation in the muscles of your lower back. Wait ten seconds before moving on (for the sake of brevity, I will omit mentioning the five and ten second counts from now on. However, make sure you include them in your practice).

Now move on to your chest. Tighten all your chest muscles. Hold it. Tighten it. Feel the tension build. Now relax. Let it go. Allow the tension to drain away. Feel the difference.

Now your stomach muscles. Tighten your abdominal muscles as though you were preparing to take a punch. Tighten. Hold. Hold. Now relax. Notice and enjoy the relaxed feelings in your stomach.

Now your right buttock. Squeeze the muscle. Hold it. Tighten it. Hold it. Now relax. Focus on the difference between the tension and the relaxation. Learn to recognize the feeling of tension so that you can let it go.

Now the left buttock. Tighten. Feel the tension build. Hold. Tighten. Hold. Now relax. Feel the relaxation.

Now your right thigh. Tighten those muscles. Hold it. Let the tension build. Hold it. Now relax. Notice the difference.

Now the left. Let the tension build. Hold it. Tighten it. Hold. Now relax. Feel the relaxation.

Next, tighten your right calf muscle by arching up your right foot. Hold. Tighten. Build. Hold. Now relax. Notice the difference.

Then do the same for your left calf. Arch up your left foot. Hold it. Build. Hold. Now relax. Let it go. Feel the relaxation in your left calf muscle.

Now tighten the muscles in your right foot and toes. Curl your toes in and squeeze. Let the tension build. Hold. Tighten. Hold. Now relax. Notice the difference.

Do the same for your left foot. Curl your toes in and squeeze. Tighten. Hold. Build. Hold. Now relax. Be aware of the sense of relaxation. Notice the difference between feeling tense and feeling relaxed.

Now review all the muscle groups of your body to see if you have any tension left in your body. If so, focus on it and relax it away. Start with your head and work down to your toes. Let go of all tension. You can use this exercise to relax away tension whenever you notice it building. Remember that when your body feels at ease, your spirit will feel at ease as well. This is the end of the Phase I variation.

Use this three-phase relaxation technique whenever you need to calm down. Remember, complete all three phases the first few times you do the exercise. After you've become skilled at doing it, you can adapt the exercise to emphasize whatever works best for you. Completing the exercise regularly will keep your stress and anger at low, manageable levels.

Teen Relaxation Tips

- Realize you cannot be relaxed and fuming at the same time, so use relaxation to drive away anger.
- Use relaxation exercises to help you control anger signs such as: rapid pulse, flushing skin, rising temperature and high blood pressure.
- Manage your stress and anger by doing relaxation exercises.
- Initiate a relaxation exercise either to calm yourself or to fall asleep.
- Use audiotapes to assist your training.
- Be aware that the formal relaxation exercise has three phases: muscle relaxation, imagery and the countdown.
- As you become more skilled, you can drop Phases I and II.
- Phase I has two variations. The first involves relaxing your muscle groups. The second involves tensing and then relaxing your muscles.
- Practice until you are able to relax your body on cue.
- Practice regularly—every day or every other day.
- Rate your tension level before and after completing the exercise.

chapter 9

What Eminem Never Learned:
Stop Pissing Everybody Off

And there's a million of us just like me
Who cuss like me; who just don't give a f*** like me.
- Eminem, "The Real Slim Shady"

Eminem's records, music videos and personal appearances have caused much controversy. His personality is outrageous and provocative. He constantly argues with everyone: fans, deejays, staff members, other performers and recording executives. One of his latest skirmishes occurred at the 2002 MTV Video Music Awards where he threatened to kick the butt of musical talent, Moby. Let Eminem's outrageous personality be a model for how you *shouldn't* behave. Don't go searching for fights the way he does. Eminem has spoken about growing up in a tough neighborhood and having to survive in that environment. You can do better than that. You can learn how to handle conflict, avoid being the focus of other people's anger and stay out of trouble. Unlike Eminem, you don't need to wait until you've become rich or famous in order to get people off your back. This chapter will teach you how to increase your self-control and handle conflicts with others.

Teen Anger Self-Control Rating

Before we continue, I want you to take a test that will gauge how well you now can control your thoughts and actions. Here are a number of questions to think about. Let's take a look at the first question together:

1. When you promise to do something, do you do it?
    Always   1   2   3   4   5   6   7   Never

Answer this question by circling one of the numbers on the scale. Notice that there is a word on either end of the scale. Circling a low number means that your answer tends toward the word on the left side of the scale. In this example, the number 1 represents the answer "always," while the number 2 means "almost always" and the number 3 means "much of the time." Circling a high number means that your answer tends toward the word on the right side of the scale. In this example, the number 7 means "never," while the number 6 means "hardly ever" and the number 5 means "not often." The number 4 will always represent a middle point—in this case, "sometimes." Now you are ready to apply your understanding of the scale to answer all of the questions:

1. When you promise to do something, do you do it?
    Always   1   2   3   4   5   6   7   Never

2. Do you butt into games or activities even when you haven't been invited?
    Never   1   2   3   4   5   6   7   Often

3. Can you deliberately calm yourself down when you're excited or wound up?
    Yes   1   2   3   4   5   6   7   No

4. Is the quality of your work always about the same or does it vary a lot?
    Same   1   2   3   4   5   6   7   Varies

5. Do you work for long-range goals?
    Yes   1   2   3   4   5   6   7   No

6. When you ask a question, do you tend to wait for an answer or do you jump to something else (e.g., a new question) before waiting for an answer?
    Wait   1   2   3   4   5   6   7   Jump

7. When talking with friends, do you tend to interrupt when some-
    one else is speaking or do you wait until it's your turn to speak?
    Wait   1   2   3   4   5   6   7   Interrupt

8. Do you stick to what you are doing until you're finished with it?
    Yes   1   2   3   4   5   6   7   No

9. Do you follow the instructions of responsible adults?
    Always   1   2   3   4   5   6   7   Never

10. Do you have to have everything right away?
    No   1   2   3   4   5   6   7   Yes

11. When you have to wait in line, do you do so patiently?
    Yes   1   2   3   4   5   6   7   No

12. Do you sit still in class?
    Yes   1   2   3   4   5   6   7   No

13. When working in a group, can you accept other people's sugges-
    tions or do you insist on imposing your own ideas on the others?
    Can accept   1   2   3   4   5   6   7   Imposes

14. Do you have to be reminded several times to do something before
    you actually do it?
    Never   1   2   3   4   5   6   7   Always

15. When reprimanded, do you answer back inappropriately?
    Never   1   2   3   4   5   6   7   Always

16. Are you accident prone?
    No   1   2   3   4   5   6   7   Yes

17. Do you neglect or forget assigned chores or tasks?
    Never   1   2   3   4   5   6   7   Always

18. Are there days when you seem incapable of settling down to do
    school or homework?
    Never   1   2   3   4   5   6   7   Often

19. If given the choice, would you prefer to accept a small present today or accept a larger one tomorrow?

    Today   1   2   3   4   5   6   7   Tomorrow

20. Do you take things that belong to others?

    Never   1   2   3   4   5   6   7   Often

21. Do you bother others when they are trying to do something?

    No   1   2   3   4   5   6   7   Yes

22. Do you break basic rules?

    Never   1   2   3   4   5   6   7   Often

23. Do you watch where you are going?

    Always   1   2   3   4   5   6   7   Never

24. When someone asks you a question, do you give one thoughtful answer or blurt out several answers all at once?

    One   1   2   3   4   5   6   7   Several
    answer   answers

25. Are you easily distracted from your work or chores?

    No   1   2   3   4   5   6   7   Yes

26. Would you describe yourself as being careful or careless?

    Careful   1   2   3   4   5   6   7   Careless

27. When you play games with friends, do you follow the rules, wait your turn and cooperate with teammates?

    Yes   1   2   3   4   5   6   7   No

28. Do you start an activity and then stick to it or do you switch from activity to activity?

    Stick to one   1   2   3   4   5   6   7   Switch

29. If you find a task to be too difficult, do you seek help or do you quit in frustration?

    Seek help   1   2   3   4   5   6   7   Quit

30. Do you disrupt games?
    Never   1   2   3   4   5   6   7   Always

31. Do you think before you act?
    Yes   1   2   3   4   5   6   7   No

32. If you paid more attention to your school work, do you think you would do much better than you do now?
    No   1   2   3   4   5   6   7   Yes

33. Do you concentrate on one thing at a time or do you do many things at once?
    One thing   1   2   3   4   5   6   7   Many things

Look over your results. Have you circled a lot of fives, sixes and sevens? If so, you probably have trouble controlling your angry thoughts and hostile emotions. Now is the time to make a change and learn how to get control of yourself. The rest of this chapter will help you to do just that.

In my practice, I like to talk about the **A-B-C**s of anger. **"A"** stands for **a**ntecedents (what comes before the anger), **"B"** stands for **b**ehavior, and **"C"** stands for **c**onsequences. You can think of these three stages in the following way:

A. What led up to your angry outburst (antecedent)?
B. What did you do (behavior)?
C. What followed as a result of your actions (consequences)?

We talked about antecedents (what provokes your anger) when we discussed triggers in chapter 6. In this chapter, we will focus on consequences or what follows after your angry outburst. If you think out ahead of time what the consequences of your angry behavior will be, you'll find it easier to control that behavior. Remember Tony and Jennifer from chapter 1? Tony found it easier to stop fighting when he remembered that this behavior would get him expelled from school. Jennifer found it easier to stop obsessing about her weight when she remembered that this behavior would endanger her health. Thinking about consequences kept them from acting in particular ways. Like Tony and Jennifer, you too will find it easier to control your anger by thinking out what the consequences of your behavior will be. To assess the consequences of your actions ask yourself this question:

If I do this now, then _____
will probably happen later.

Any action will have both short- and long-term consequences. It's often easy to see the short-term consequences of your hostile behavior; it is more difficult but more important to work on considering long-term consequences when you get angry:

Short-term: "If I slug him now, he'll shut up."

Long-term: "If I slug him now, my probation will probably get extended three months."

Do you see the difference between the two? Do you see how thinking about long-term consequences will be more persuasive in getting you to change your behavior?

Anger Consequences Exercise

Think of some aggressive or angry acts you have committed in the last two months. What were the short-term consequences of those actions? What were the long-term consequences? Write them down in the list which follows.

Act #1: What did you do? _____

_____

What were the short-term consequences? _____

_____

_____

What were the long-term consequences? _____

_____

_____

Act #2: What did you do? _____

_____

What were the short-term consequences? _____

_____

_____

What were the long-term consequences? _____
_____
_____

Act #3: What did you do? _____
_____

What were the short-term consequences? _____
_____
_____

What were the long-term consequences? _____
_____
_____

Serious Consequences Exercise

Some of the consequences of our angry acts are more serious than others. In the space that follows, write down an angry act that you have committed in the last two months. Then list as many consequences of that act as you can think of, starting with the least serious and working toward the most serious.

Angry Act:_____
_____

Least serious: _____
_____
_____

Most serious: _____
_____
_____

We can distinguish between three different types of consequences. Sometimes the consequences of our actions affect our life situations, such as getting detention/suspended from school, being sent back to court or being ordered to enter an anger management program or a facility. I call these "external" consequences. Sometimes the consequences affect how we feel about ourselves, such as losing self-respect or feeling badly. I call these "internal" consequences. Sometimes the consequences affect our relationships with others, such as losing friends or being excluded from a group or team. I call these "social" consequences.

Consequences Exercise

Think about some angry acts that you have committed. Write down some of the external, internal and social consequences that resulted from your behavior.

External_____

_____

Internal _____

_____

Social_____

_____

Now imagine that, instead of acting out in anger, you had controlled yourself in that moment. Write down some examples of how applying this control could influence the consequences of your behavior for the better:

External_____

_____

Internal _____

_____

Social_____

_____

In the next pages are ten step-by-step skills that will teach you how to reduce conflict in your life. Use these skills whenever the appropriate moment arises. If you adopt these procedures rather than lashing out in anger, you will find your personal relationships and life experiences greatly improved.

Teen Anger Skills for Reducing Conflict

Skill 1. How to Express a Complaint

Follow these steps whenever you want to complain to someone about something:

1. Define in your mind what the problem is and who is responsible for it.
2. Think of ways the problem might be solved.
3. Tell the person to whom you are making the complaint what the problem is and how it might be solved.
4. Ask for a response.
5. Show that you understand his or her feelings.
6. Come to an agreement on the steps to be taken by each of you.

Skill 2. How to Respond to Someone Else's Feelings
If you want other people to understand how you feel, first you must understand how they feel. Follow these steps whenever you want to understand how someone else is feeling:
1. Observe the other person's words, facial expressions, body language and actions.
2. Think about what the other person might be feeling and how strong those feelings are.
3. Decide whether it would be helpful to let the other person know you understand his or her feelings.
4. Tell the other person, in a caring and sincere manner, how you think he or she is feeling.

Skill 3. How to Prepare for a Stressful Conversation
Sometimes you can't avoid uncomfortable conversations with your parents, teachers or peers. If you follow these steps beforehand, you'll find these conversations to be a lot less stressful.
1. Picture yourself in the stressful situation before you enter it.
2. Think about how you will feel and why you will feel that way.
3. Imagine the other person in the stressful situation. Think about how that person will feel and why.
4. Go over in your mind what you want to tell the other person.
5. Imagine what he or she will say in response.
6. Repeat the above steps using as many different approaches to the conversation as you can imagine.
7. Choose the best approach and use it when you enter the situation.

Skill 4. How to Respond to Anger
What do you do when someone gets angry with you? In the future, follow these easy steps to help deal with the situation and reduce the other person's anger.
1. Stay calm and listen openly to what the other person has to say.

2. Show that you understand what the other person is feeling.
3. Ask the other person to explain anything you do not understand.
4. Show that you understand *why* the other person feels angry.
5. If it is appropriate, express your thoughts and feelings about the situation.

Skill 5. How to Keep Out of Fights

Physical violence never solves anything. Instead of fighting, follow these steps the next time you want to throw a punch.

1. Stop and think about why you want to fight.
2. Decide what you want to happen in the long run.
3. Think about other ways to handle the situation besides fighting.
4. Decide on the best way to handle the situation and do it.

Skill 6. How to Help Others

1. Consider why the other person might need or want your help.
2. Think of the ways you could be more helpful.
3. Ask the other person if he or she needs or wants your help.
4. Tell the other person your ideas for how you can be more helpful.
5. Help the other person.

Skill 7. How to Deal with an Accusation

1. Think about what the other person has accused you of doing.
2. Think about why the person might have accused you.
3. Think about ways to answer the person's accusations.
4. Choose the best way and do it.

Skill 8. How to Deal with Group Pressure

1. Think about what the other people want you to do and why.
2. Decide what you want to do.
3. Decide how to tell the other people what you want to do.
4. Tell the group what you have decided.

Skill 9. How to Express Affection

1. Decide if you have good feelings about the other person.
2. Decide whether or not you think the other person would like to know about your feelings.
3. Think about the different ways in which you might best express your feelings.

4. Choose the right time and place to express your feelings.
5. Express affection in a warm and caring manner.

Skill 10. How to Respond to Failure
1. Decide whether or not you have failed.
2. Think about both the personal reasons and the circumstances that caused you to fail.
3. Decide how you might do things differently if you tried again.
4. Decide if you want to try again.
5. If it is appropriate, try again, using your revised approach.

Teen Anger Prescription for Dealing with Provocation

If you feel as though someone may try to provoke you to anger, prepare for the moment beforehand by thinking these thoughts:

- *This is going to upset me, but I know how to deal with it.*
- *I can work out a plan to handle this.*
- *I can manage the situation. I know how to regulate my anger.*
- *If I find myself getting upset, I'll know what to do.*
- *There won't be any need for an argument.*
- *Try not to take this too seriously.*
- *This could be a testy situation, but I believe in myself.*
- *Time for me to take a few deep breaths of relaxation.*
- *I should feel comfortable, relaxed and at ease.*
- *Easy does it. Remember to keep my sense of humor.*

Teen Anger Prescription for Dealing with Confrontation

Before you have a confrontation with someone, prepare for it by going over these tips in your mind:

- *Stay calm. Just continue to relax.*
- *As long as I keep my cool, I'm in control.*
- *Just roll with the punches; don't get bent out of shape.*
- *Can I come out of this confrontation with something positive?*
- *I don't need to prove myself.*
- *There is no point in getting mad.*
- *I must not make more out of this than I have to.*
- *I'm not going to let her get to me.*
- *There may be many reasons why he's acting this way. I shouldn't jump to conclusions and assume the worst.*
- *It's really a shame she has to act like this.*
- *For someone to be that irritable, he must be awfully unhappy.*

- *If I start to get mad, I'll just be banging my head against the wall. So I might as well just relax.*
- *There is no need to doubt myself. What he says does not matter.*
- *I'm on top of this situation and it's under control.*

Teen Anger Prescription for Dealing With Angry Feelings

It's okay to feel angry—just don't act out irrationally on your anger. Learn to control how you feel by repeating these thoughts in your mind:

- *My muscles are starting to feel tight. Time to relax and slow things down.*
- *Getting upset won't help.*
- *It's just not worth it to get so angry.*
- *I'll let him make a fool of himself.*
- *I have a right to be annoyed, but I'm going to keep a lid on it.*
- *Time to take a deep breath.*
- *Let's take the issue point by point.*
- *My anger is a signal of what I need to do. Time to calm down.*
- *I'm not going to get pushed around, but I'm not going to go haywire either.*
- *Maybe I can reason this problem out with her.*
- *Maybe I can get him to work with me. It could be that we're both right.*
- *Negatives lead to more negatives. Work constructively.*
- *He would probably like me to get really angry. Well, I'm going to disappoint him.*
- *I can't expect people to act the way I want them to.*
- *Take it easy, do not get pushy.*

Teen Anger Prescription for After the Provocation and Confrontation

Sometimes when you are provoked or confronted, the situation will end without a good resolution. When that happens, do not get upset. Instead, think about what went wrong and how you can do things differently next time. Before you can do that, you may need to go over these insights in your mind:

- *I shouldn't dwell on it right now. Worrying about it will only make me more upset.*
- *I'll think about this later when I've calmed down.*

◆ *This is a difficult situation and it will take time to straighten it out.*

◆ *I should shake this off. I don't want it to interfere with my school work.*

◆ *I'll get better at dealing with this kind of situation when I get more practice.*

◆ *I should perform a relaxation exercise right now. It's impossible to feel relaxed and angry at the same time.*

◆ *Maybe I should laugh about it. It's probably not as serious as I think.*

◆ *I refuse to take this personally.*

◆ *Let me take a deep breath.*

If you've managed to resolve the conflict successfully, congratulate yourself by thinking some of the following positive thoughts:

◆ *I handled that one pretty well. It worked!*

◆ *That wasn't as hard as I thought.*

◆ *It could have been a lot worse.*

◆ *I could have gotten more upset than it was worth.*

◆ *I actually got through that without getting angry.*

◆ *I'm better off when I don't take things too seriously.*

◆ *I guess I've been getting upset for too long when it wasn't even necessary.*

◆ *I'm doing better at this all the time.*

On the following pages, you will find two worksheets to help you express your anger in more constructive ways. One is a Conflict Log and the other is an Anger Journal. Make copies of these Log pages and use them whenever you get angry. Keep track of how you respond to anger-producing situations. If you write in the Log and the Journal regularly, you will begin to notice changes in your behavior as you manage your anger better. Just by writing about your anger, you will understand it better and this will help you change your behavior. By expressing yourself in words, you keep yourself from acting out on your negative emotions. Monitor yourself during or after each anger situation by using the Conflict Log and the Anger Journal.

CONFLICT LOG

Date: _____

Where were you?

Home	Bedroom	Kitchen	Family Room
Dorm	Bathroom	At Work	Classroom
Gym	Dining Room	Outside	School Hallway

Other: _____

What Happened?

Somebody teased me/insulted me.　　　Somebody did something I didn't like.
Somebody took something of mine.　　　I did something wrong.
Somebody told me to do something.　　　Somebody started fighting with me.
Other: _____

Who did you get angry with?

Friend	Parent	Teacher	Another adult
Brother/Sister	Fellow student	Neighbor	Stranger

Other: _____

What did you do?

Hit the other person	Ran away	Ignored it	Used Anger Mgmt.
Told a friend	Cried	Yelled	Broke something
Was restrained	Told teacher	Talked it out	Walked away calmly

Other: _____

How did you handle yourself?

1	2	3	4	5
Poorly	Not so well	Okay	Good	Great

How angry were you?

Burning	Very angry	Moderately angry	Mildly angry	Not angry

ANGER JOURNAL

Date: _____

Rate how angry you feel/felt on a scale of one to ten, one being not angry at all and ten being extremely irate:

1   2   3   4   5   6   7   8   9   10

What sensations did you feel before you got angry?_____
_____
_____

What thoughts were you thinking before you got angry? _____
_____
_____

How were you acting before you got angry? _____
_____
_____

Were you under the influence of alcohol or drugs? ____ **Yes** ____ **No**

What provoked you to get angry?_____
_____
_____

Did you take a Time Out? ____ **Yes** ____ **No**

If you did take a Time Out, how did it go? _____
_____
_____

Write down how you feel at this very moment:
Right now, I feel _____
_____
_____
_____
_____
_____
_____

Teen Anger Tips

- Let Eminem be a model for how you *shouldn't* act.
- Remember '**A-B-C**': every angry action has **A**ntecedents, finds expression in **B**ehavior, and then has **C**onsequences.
- If you think ahead to the possible consequences of your actions, you may be able to stop yourself from committing those actions.
- Think: *If I do this now,* _____ *will probably happen later.*
- Our actions often have short-term and long-term consequences.
- Some consequences are more serious than others.
- External consequences are those that alter your relationship with the world.
- Internal consequences are those that affect how you think about yourself.
- Social consequences are those that affect your relationship with other people.
- Remember that anger will produce negative consequences and self-control will produce positive ones.
- Use the ten skills of reducing conflict.
- If you prepare yourself for provocation and confrontation, you will deal with the situation more effectively.
- Use positive thoughts to deal with your anger.
- Think positively when you reflect back on your angry confrontation.
- Get into the habit of writing in the Anger Journal every time you get angry.
- Remember that writing in a journal changes your behavior, because it forces you to express your anger in a more productive way.

chapter 10

It's Easier to Control
Your Thoughts than Your Hormones

It's just another day, that didn't go my way.
It's just another day
'Cause times change, your mind's rearranged.
- Mest, "Another Day"

Adolescent years are often a time of turmoil. This is natural and common. Emotionally, you are no longer a child but are not yet an adult. This "in-between" stage can be a confusing time for both you and your family. No doubt your relationship with your family has already changed significantly. You are probably pushing for more freedom while your parents are pulling back, trying to keep you within certain limits. At the same time, your body is changing, requiring other adjustments. Your glands are pumping out large quantities of new hormones. These hormones have a powerful effect on your moods and emotions. Although such emotional and physiological changes are natural in adolescence, they can be difficult to live through.

Many teens become seriously depressed during this period but do not even know what they are experiencing. It is hard enough to recognize depression in adults, no less teens. The warning signs can include changes in sleep, appetite, motivation, concentration, memory, low self-esteem, apathy, sadness, fatigue, loss of interest in activities and an inability to feel pleasure. Depression can also be identified by decreased activity, isolation, negative thoughts about others and oneself, hopelessness, helplessness, and suicidal thoughts and attempts. It's very hard to recognize depression in adolescents, because it can manifest itself in unexpected ways, such as irritability, anger, aggressive behavior, acting out on emotions, underachievement at school, disinterest in activities like sports that were once enjoyed, self-medication through alcohol and drug use and self-destructiveness (risk-taking, sabotaging oneself, even self-mutilation).

Anger is closely related to depression—depression has been described as the turning of anger against the self. Adolescents who are depressed must also deal with hormonal changes that wreck havoc with their emotions. Depression is a serious subject and we will address it more fully in another chapter. For now, I only want to talk about the intensified emotions that all adolescents have to deal with. I'll teach you how to cope with these emotions effectively.

As the title of this chapter indicates, thoughts are easier to control than hormones. Remember, you can't do anything to affect the hormonal changes that you are undergoing during your adolescence. These hormonal changes do a lot to affect your emotions, which in turn affect your thoughts and behavior. Although you cannot control your hormones and emotions, you *can* control what you think and how you act. Moreover, changing your thoughts and behavior can have an indirect effect on your emotional state. Researchers have found that changes in thought and behavior can alter the activity of a person's brain. Brain scans show that human beings are consciously able to slow down activity in certain parts of their brains. Medication and therapy have been known to produce the same results. This is an important fact, because it shows that changes in thought and behavior can affect the physical state of your brain and can achieve the same results as medication. In this chapter, we will discuss how you can make those changes.

Believe it or not, the human brain is wired in such a way that it is impossible for us to think of more than one thing at a time. When I tell this to my patients, many of them don't believe me at first. Recall from chapter 1 my client, Jennifer, a highly intelligent girl who tended to have repetitive, rapid-fire thoughts involving her obsession with weight. She was sure that she was able to think about more than one thing at a time. I convinced her that this perception was wrong, that it only seemed that way because her brain was bouncing so rapidly from one thought to another. Once she grasped this, she set about trying to control her thoughts. Although she had to stop herself from obsessing over her weight, she eventually was able to control her self-destructive behavior. She found it easier to exert this control the more she practiced. At first, Jennifer had hoped to find a magical "cure" which would eliminate her body image problem. Unfortunately, there are no magical cures in therapy. But what Jennifer *did* find were skills that helped her cope with distress and manage her problems effectively. You can acquire these skills as well. Learning them will take hard work and some mental effort, as you no doubt have realized by now. But the hard work and effort will be worth it. I have seen many teens turn their lives around with these skills and I know that you can, too.

Sometimes we may feel as though we can think of more than one thing at a time. However, this is not the case. When we feel this way, what actually happens is that our brain jumps back and forth between many different thoughts very rapidly. This creates the illusion of thinking of more than one thing at a time. Once you realize that you can only think one thing at a time, you will find it easier to control your thoughts.

At times we can control our thoughts so effectively that it seems as though we are not thinking about anything at all—we become totally and completely involved in whatever we are doing at the time. As actors say, we become lost "in the moment"—athletes call it being "in the zone." These experiences happen rarely and are lost whenever we call attention to them. We call these moments "peak" experiences. These experiences are to be cherished and sought after. For example, there have been times when I've been working with patients and have "lost myself" in intense concentration. Time slipped by without my even noticing it. Perhaps you can think of a time in your life when you have felt this way as well. Such examples, I hope, will show you that, if you can learn to focus on whatever you are doing at the moment you are doing it, your angry thoughts and emotions will calm down.

While I was writing this book, for example, I became so enthusiastic about it that I found myself feeling impatient while spending time with my family. I wanted so much to return to my writing. When I recognized this, I decided to change my way of thinking. I decided to focus on my family while I was with them and focus on my book while I was working on that. I told myself that being impatient with my family while we were together was not the way I wanted to act. By changing my attitude, I felt more relaxed with my family and the quality of our time together improved. I controlled my thoughts, which, in turn, affected my feelings and behavior.

Just as I did, you can learn how to change your angry thoughts and thus change your hostile emotions and behavior. Remember though, we first must identify the thoughts that *need* changing *before* we can change them. Earlier I pointed out some thoughts we often have when we get angry:

- *He did this purposely.*
- *She did this to spite me.*
- *He did this to make me look like a fool.*
- *If I slug him, he'll shut up.*

Sometimes these thoughts accurately describe the situation at hand. But, more often than not, they don't—they are merely false assumptions made in the heat of the moment. When our passions get the best of us, we often make faulty leaps in logic and reasoning. Thoughts such as these are called "irrational." You need to recognize when your anger is leading you to think irrationally. Using this recognition will help you change your behavior for the better.

There are different categories of **irrational thinking**:

1. **Over-generalization.** You view a single negative event as part of a never-ending pattern of defeat: *Things always happen this way. It never changes.* Common words: always, never, forever.

2. **Catastrophic thinking.** You see events as being more tragic or horrible than they really are: *This is the worst thing that could happen to me—my life is ruined.* Common words: horrible, incredibly awful, tragic, etc.

3. **"Should" statements.** You think that people "should" act in a certain way and are disappointed when they don't: *He should know how I feel when I act this way.* You think things "should" be a certain way and get frustrated when they're not: *I have to get this done today or else.* Common words: should, must, ought to and have to.

4. **Black-or-white thinking.** You look at things in "all or nothing" categories that focus on extremes: *He is the absolute worst teacher I've ever had!* Common words: love/hate, best/worst, wonderful/terrible, etc.

5. **Blaming.** You assign blame to yourself or to others after an unpleasant situation: *You should have known better—it's all your fault.*

6. **Labeling.** You assign a label when you or someone else makes a mistake: *I'm a jerk. You're a loser.*

In order to change this faulty behavior, you must substitute a rational thought for each irrational thought. Let's look at our six categories of **rational thinking**, one by one:

1. Instead of over-generalizing, restrict your thoughts and feelings to the specific situation that you are in: *Well, it didn't work out* this *time.*

2. Don't automatically assume that everything and anything that happens in your life is a catastrophe. Keep things in perspective.

Stay away from extreme descriptions like "horrible" and "tragic"; use more moderate words like "unfortunate" and "unpleasant": *This is unfortunate. I'm beginning to feel sad.*

3. Don't form unreasonable expectations of how other people "should" behave. Be realistic: *It's better for him to act differently, but what he does is up to him. I can't control him.* Likewise, don't think you can dictate to the world what "should" happen. Instead, talk about what you *want* or *would like* to happen. Recognize that things may not work out the way you want them to: *I want to get this done today, but I realize that I may not.*

4. Don't think in terms of black and white—don't think in extremes. Pay attention to the middle ground. Look for positives in any situation: *That teacher is really boring, but at least he cares about us and always tries his best.*

5. Don't automatically assign blame when something bad happens. Sometimes no one is to blame. Even if someone is at fault, it's rarely helpful to point that out. Look to see how the situation can be improved: *Okay, this is an unfortunate situation. Mistakes happen. What can we do to fix it?*

6. Don't assign a *permanent* label to describe what happened in a *passing* moment. Focus on what occurred, not on the character of the person involved: *I made a mistake* or *You got it wrong this time, but next time you'll do better.*

Teen Irrational Thought Correction Exercise

Make a list of any irrational thoughts you've had when you've been angry. Then write down another way to react which will change the irrational thoughts into rational ones.

Example:

Irrational thought: *Mom forgot to pick me up after school out of spite.*

Rational thought: *Mom wasn't trying to spite me when she forgot to pick me up after school. She probably forgot because she's been so preoccupied with her own stress lately.*

1) Irrational thought: _____

_____

Rational thought: _____

_____

2) Irrational thought: _____

_____

Rational thought: _____

_____

3) Irrational thought: _____

_____

Rational thought: _____

_____

4) Irrational thought: _____

_____

Rational thought: _____

_____

5) Irrational thought: _____

_____

Rational thought: _____

_____

As we've seen, many of our irrational thoughts are based on what we think *should, ought to* or *must* happen: *She must stay out of my room and stop going through my things.* We can make those thoughts rational by expressing them as a preference: *I would prefer it if she stayed out of my room and left my stuff alone.* If you can learn to express your preference rather than dictating the way things 'should' be, you will reduce your anger significantly.

The problem is that each individual has his or her own ideal of how reality should be. When our ideals conflict with another's, we need to understand the other person's point of view. It doesn't have to be a matter of one person being right and the other being wrong. It may simply be a difference of opinion or viewpoint: you think one way, but I think another. It's much easier to understand how a person thinks than it is to beat them into submission with an argument. If you understand where the other person is coming from, you will be better prepared to resolve the conflict between the two of you peacefully.

Teen Anger Exercise

As we all do, you probably have many ideas about how things "should," "ought" or "must" be. In the following exercise, list them. Then change each statement into one expressing your idea as a preference.

Example Should, Ought, Must: *My brother should stop interrupting me.*
Preference: *I would prefer that my brother stop interrupting me.*

1) Should, Ought, Must: _____

Preference: _____

_____

2) Should, Ought, Must: _____

Preference: _____

_____

3) Should, Ought, Must: _____

Preference: _____

_____

4) Should, Ought, Must: _____

Preference: _____

_____

5) Should, Ought, Must: _____

Preference: _____

_____

This chapter has focused on discussing how to change angry thoughts, but sometimes that's not so easy to do. When you find yourself in these situations, it may be better to simply distract yourself from your angry thoughts. You might do this by listening to music or talk radio, watching television, picking up a magazine or book or other similar activities. You might even distract yourself by calling to mind pleasant memories or experiences from your past. When you distract yourself, be on guard against anger creeping back into your thoughts. If you find yourself becoming angry again, redouble your efforts to find something new to distract and refocus yourself.

Teen Anger Exercise

What activities do you enjoy the most? What activities will you turn to when you want to distract yourself from your anger? List them.

1) _____

2) _____

3) _____

4) _____

5) _____

6) _____

7) _____

8) _____

9) _____

10) _____

Teen Anger Exercise

What are your most pleasant memories or experiences? What memories will you use to distract yourself from your anger? List them.

1) _____

2) _____

3) _____

4) _____

5) _____

6) _____

7) _____

8) _____

9) _____

10) _____

If you find that these methods are not enough to distract yourself from anger, you should consider using another technique called "thought stopping." Here you simply say or think *STOP!* whenever an angry thought intrudes. You might even wear a rubber band around your wrist and snap it whenever you say *STOP!* to yourself.

You might also borrow a technique from our relaxation exercise. Remember, you have more control over your thoughts when you are calmer. Say "calm" as you inhale through your nose and say "peace" as you exhale through your mouth. Keep your breathing even. Doing this exercise will relax your body and give your mind something to focus on other than your angry thoughts.

Teen Anger Tips

- ◆ Adolescence is naturally a time of turmoil.
- ◆ Your body is changing in significant ways.
- ◆ Your body is now producing hormones which can powerfully influence your moods and emotions.
- ◆ You can't control these hormonal changes, but you can control your thoughts.
- ◆ Changes in thought and behavior can have as much effect on the brain as medication.
- ◆ We can only think one thing at a time.
- ◆ Choose what you think.
- ◆ Control the things you think or say to yourself in your head.
- ◆ By controlling your thoughts, you will change your emotions and your behavior.
- ◆ Moments of passion can lead us to think irrational thoughts.
- ◆ Learn to replace those irrational thoughts with rational ones.
- ◆ Don't use the words "should," "ought" and "must" when what you really mean to do is express a preference.
- ◆ If you can't control your angry thoughts, distract yourself from them.
- ◆ Tell yourself *STOP!* to help silence angry thoughts.
- ◆ Say "calm" as you inhale and "peace" as you exhale to reduce your anger.

chapter 11

Don't Trust Anyone Over the Age of Twenty-five Part I: Communicating with the Enemy

I have nothing to say
But I feel like my mouth is open wide.
- Ill Nino, "What Comes Around"

"Communication"—it's a word most of us think we know and under-stand. After all, we "communicate" every day, don't we? However, the reality behind communication is not as simple as it first seems. The process involves several hidden steps that make it more complicated than we might suspect. First of all, someone must have a thought that he or she would like to disclose. Then that person must try to express the thought in words—sometimes those words will clearly express that thought, sometimes not. Next, the person who hears those words must attempt to understand them—sometimes that understanding will be clear and accurate, sometimes not. Then the second person must think of a response and express the response in words. Thus the process repeats itself.

As you can see, the process can be entangled and leaves many oppor-tunities along the way for the wrong message to be sent or received. What you say may not clearly express what you think, and what some-one hears may not accurately represent what you've said. A great many other factors may also obscure communication. For example, we may get so focused on what we want to say that we don't really listen to what someone else is saying or we are distracted by nonverbal forms of communication like facial expressions or body language. At other times, we are too emotional to express ourselves effectively. Sometimes we radically disagree with another person in our perception of the same thing. No wonder communication can often be a complete mess! But there is hope. In this chapter, we will discuss skills that will help you bypass these obstacles and communicate more effectively.

Types of Miscommunication

When people miscommunicate, they tend to do so in recognizable ways. Here are fourteen common ways that people fail to communicate effectively. When you have read them, ask yourself if you are prone to this kind of behavior.

1. **Explaining yourself too soon.** Attempting to justify yourself before acknowledging how the other person feels.
   A: "I'm mad because you blew me off in the middle of our conversation."
   B: "Yeah, but I did that because you weren't making any sense."
   This sends the message: *You have no right to feel the way you do.*

2. **Arguing against someone's feelings.** Attempting to dispute or reassure another's feelings instead of simply accepting what they have to say.
   A: "You made me mad yesterday."
   B: "There's no reason for you to be mad."
   This sends the message: *You're wrong to feel the way you do.*

3. **Condescending.** Putting yourself in a superior position and looking down on how another person feels. Sometimes you can convey this simply through the tone of your voice.
   This sends the message: *I'm strong and smart, you're weak and pitiful.*

4. **Blackmailing.** Avoiding the issue at hand by falsely claiming that the other person has gone too far.
   A: "You can't control your anger."
   B: "Won't you ever stop? All this criticism is giving me a headache!"
                                    OR
      "If you're saying this purposely to get me depressed, then you've succeeded."
   This sends the message: *I'm so sensitive and you're a jerk.*

5. **Responding too soon.** Jumping in to apologize before the other person has fully expressed him/herself.

> A: "What you said made me feel— "
> B: "I know what you're going to say and I'm really sorry."

This sends the message: *I understand how you feel better than you do* and *Don't bother talking—I'm too impatient to listen.*

6. **Interrupting.** Cutting off the other person before he or she can finish a thought.

> A: "What I want to say is—"
> B: "Why do you act like you're so important? I hate it when..." etc., etc.

This sends the message: *What I have to say is more important than what you have to say.*

7. **Punishing.** Describing the other person's behavior in the most accusatory way possible.

> A: "I didn't mean to hurt you."
> B: "I don't care! You acted like a complete monster who doesn't have an ounce of human kindness in your whole body! You're the worst!"

This sends the message: *Your apology is useless; I'll make you sorry you ever did that to me.*

8. **Pretending to be stupid.** Falsely claiming not to know what is going on.

> A: "You hurt my feelings with what you said just now."
> B: "Huh? I don't know what you're talking about."

This sends the message: *I don't care to understand you, so shut up already.*

9. **Passing the buck.** Shifting responsibility for the problem over to the other person, rather than trying to help out or assume responsibility yourself.

> A: "Sometimes when I get angry at you, I can't express myself properly."
> B: "Well, that's your problem."

This sends the message: *Nothing's my fault; everything is your fault. I'm not interested in working this out with you.*

10. **Intellectualizing the problem.** Avoiding responding to someone's emotions by turning the discussion into an intellectual conversation on the same subject.

    A: "I get mad when you don't call me."

    B: "Yeah, some people are like that. Why do you suppose that is?"

This sends the message: *I can't deal with your feelings; I'd rather generalize this issue by talking about ideas.*

11. **Playing lawyer.** Arguing over minor details in order to avoid the larger issue.

    A: "You called me a jerk yesterday."

    B: "No, I never said 'jerk.' I did not use that word. Why are you distorting the truth?"

This sends the message: *Make sure you get every minor fact right because I'd rather fight you down to the bitter end on each little detail then work through our problems.*

12. **Playing Comedian.** Turning the whole thing into a joke. You disregard another person's feelings by trying to laugh off his/her legitimate concerns.

    A: "What you just said hurt me."

    B: "Oh, lighten up, already. It's not a big deal."

This sends the message: *I don't take your feelings seriously. You're being a baby.*

13. **Scolding.** Dismissing what someone says by objecting to how he/she says it or denying his/her right to say it.

    A: "I'm upset with you because you treated me like dirt yesterday!"

    B: "Don't use that tone of voice with me! This conversation's over!"

OR

    "That's rude! I can't talk to someone who would say something like that!"

This sends the message: *You're an obnoxious person who has no right to feel the way you do. How I feel is more important.*

14. **Inattention, Spacing Out or Not Listening.** This is self-explanatory.

    A: "So what I feel is—"

    B: "Sorry, what did you say? My mind wandered there for a bit."

This sends the message: *You bore me. You're wasting my time.*

If any of these fourteen types of miscommunication seem familiar to you, try to avoid them when communicating with others.

Sometimes when people try to work out their problems, they get hung up in an endless debate over who is right and who is wrong. I see this frequently in my practice. I counsel my patients that "right" and "wrong" are meaningless and unimportant terms in counseling. What *is* important is understanding how the other person feels and working together to resolve the issue.

The way we feel can influence the way we perceive the world. This is why several different witnesses to the same event can describe that event in conflicting ways. Sometimes arguments boil down to two people differing in their perception of the same thing. In cases like these, it's foolish to argue over which perception is "right" and which is "wrong." There are no objective answers. I've had patients tell me they wanted to put a video camera in their home and tape what goes on between them and their families. Then, they said, they could show me the tape so I could judge "objectively" who is to blame for the family's problems. My answer: Save the videotape. Rather than trying to find out who's the "good guy" and who's the "bad guy," families should focus on solving their problems by improving their communication skills.

Another problem in communication can occur when two people argue with each other but are not even talking about the same thing. One person will argue one point and the other person will argue a different point, neither of them listening to the other. I see this quite often in family counseling. Sometimes I will let family members argue with one another during sessions. I call these arguments "enactments" and I let them unfold so that I can see more closely how the family communicates with each other. Of course, I never allow these arguments to go on too long—I don't want someone getting so angry that he or she leaves the session altogether! During an enactment, I try to empathize with the feelings of everyone involved. Most importantly, I watch out for the times when the family argues over completely different things.

An example of this kind of behavior occurred in a session with a girl named Amy and her parents. I let their argument go on for a little while and noticed that the two sides were talking about two entirely different things. Amy said, "You don't give me enough freedom. I can't do the things I want to do." Her parents responded, "You're lucky to live the life you do. You have a hundred times more liberties than we did at your age. We've worked hard to give you a good life and you don't appreciate it."

Do you see how the two sides are arguing over different issues? Amy was talking about her lack of freedom, but her parents were talking about her lack of appreciation. This argument could have gone on forever, because the two sides refused to talk about the same thing.

Our talks helped Amy and her parents to listen to each other. Amy's parents listened to their daughter's objections and backed off from their controlling ways. Amy listened to her parents' grievances and learned to appreciate them more. I'll return to this case later in the book. For now, the important thing is to understand how two sides need to discuss the same thing at the same time in order to communicate effectively.

In my practice, I've found that often people use some feelings to cover over other feelings that they don't want others to see. For example, many of my clients use anger to mask the fact that they really feel sad or hurt underneath. It's safer to feel angry, because allowing yourself to feel sad or hurt leaves you vulnerable. If you tell someone that he or she has hurt you, then that person might go on and hurt you further. Many people are afraid to take this risk. I don't want you to be among them. Learn to delve beneath your anger and get in touch with the hurt feelings underneath. Learn to express those hurt feelings, despite the risk. Although there's a slight chance that you'll be hurt further, more often than not you'll be reassured and comforted.

An exercise to help reinforce this point is to imagine that you've gone to your dad to discuss a serious problem. Imagine that he's sitting on the couch watching television while talking to you. Would this make you angry? If so, you'd probably feel angry because you felt hurt—hurt that your dad didn't think your problems were serious enough to distract him from the television. Rather than expressing your anger, you should express your hurt. Instead of getting angry, say: "Dad, it hurts me that you can't give my problems your full attention." This is hard to do, because we fear that we'll get an answer like: "Well, this program is more interesting than you are." But the people who care about us will never answer this way. More than likely, you'll get an answer like: "Oh, I'm sorry! I didn't realize it was so serious. I'll turn the television off right now." If you learn to express the hurt that underlies your anger, you'll stand an excellent chance of having others recognize and meet your needs.

I hope this chapter has given you some ideas about how to communicate more effectively. However, some communication problems are too complicated to be solved by simple methods, because they often involve emotionally laden subjects. In these cases, we need to introduce new skills and exercises to our conversations with others.

Floor Exercise

When your family members talk, do they shout without listening to each other? Do arguments spiral out of control? If so, then this exercise is for you. It will teach everyone in your family to listen when someone else is talking. To start, have everyone sit down in chairs that have been drawn in a circle to face each other. Turn off the television, don't answer the phone, and don't let anything distract you from this exercise. Find a soft object like a pillow to pass back and forth—don't use a hard object, because we don't want people hurling it at one another. Discuss with your family allowing no one to talk unless he or she holds the pillow. Holding the pillow gives that person the right to talk without interruption until he or she is finished and passes the pillow to someone else. The pillow cannot be taken away—it remains in that person's control until he/she is ready to give it up. Remember: a person may not talk unless he or she has the pillow. Don't interrupt. Listen! Have your family undertake this exercise twice a week for one hour. Although you might be surprised to hear it, this exercise can actually be a lot of fun. More importantly, it teaches people to change their behavior. Your family members will learn to listen to one another and not interrupt. This skill will dramatically increase your family's ability to communicate effectively with each other.

Paraphrasing Exercise

Once your family has mastered that skill, you can move on to a more complicated technique called the "Paraphrasing Exercise." Use this skill to deal with controversial or heated topics. This technique will keep conversation under control and often prevents the need for a Time Out. It takes a lot of concentration to do it correctly, but if you and your family master the paraphrasing exercise, I guarantee the number of your arguments with each other will drastically decrease. What this exercise does is slow down communication to a single thought or sentence at a time. Once someone utters a thought, the other person must repeat back what he or she has understood the first person to have said. This is what "paraphrasing" means—you take someone else's thought and express it in your own words. After this happens, the first person must indicate whether or not the paraphrase is accurate. Did the other person understand you correctly? If so, say so. Here's an example of how the exercise works:

A: I get angry whenever I come to your house and Ed is there.

B: Okay, so what you're saying is that you get mad whenever you visit me and see Ed.

A: That's right.

That was a pretty straightforward example. However, not all communication is this straightforward. It's easy for people to miscommunicate and misunderstand one another. Sometimes what we say doesn't really express what we think and sometimes what we hear doesn't really represent what was said. When we paraphrase, we make sure that we've understood the other person *perfectly*. If you feel that someone has paraphrased your words incorrectly, point that out:

A: I get angry whenever I come to your house and find Ed hanging out there.

B: Okay, so what you're saying is that you don't want me to hang out with Ed anymore.

A: No, that's not it. I don't care if you hang out with Ed. I just don't want you to hang out with him while I'm there.

B: So you mean that you don't want me to invite Ed to visit when I've invited you to my house.

A: That's it.

Do not continue the conversation until the paraphrase is successful. Once that happens, the second person may then respond to the first person's original remark. Again, the second person must limit him/herself to a single thought or sentence. Then the process begins again: the first person will paraphrase *those* words, and the second person will indicate whether or not the paraphrase is correct:

B: Well, it's stupid that you don't want to hang out with Ed.

A: You're saying that I'm stupid, because I don't like Ed.

B: No, that's not what I meant! Sorry, I shouldn't have used the word "stupid." What I meant was: I don't understand why you don't want to hang out with Ed.

A: Okay, so you don't get why I have such a problem when I come to your house and see Ed there.

B: Yeah, that's it.

Do you see how the paraphrase clarified the discussion? If Person A hadn't taken the time to paraphrase B's words, the conversation would have gotten hung up over the word "stupid." Person A probably would have thought, *Well, B thinks I'm stupid for feeling the way I do!* and felt insulted, even though B intended no insult. Then the argument might have spiraled out of control. Fortunately, the paraphrase kept the conversation on track by ensuring that both people understood one another correctly.

If you are still unsure how to do the Paraphrasing Exercise, just follow this format:

Paraphrasing Exercise Rules

Person A: Make a statement. Limit yourself to a single thought, idea or feeling. Keep it to one sentence.

Person B: Paraphrase. Translate what you've heard into your own words. Try as hard as you can to understand exactly what **A** has said.

Person A: Indicate whether or not **B**'s paraphrase was correct. If **B** has understood you, say "Yes, that's right" and move on to the next step. If **B** has not understood you, say "No, that's not it" and try to express yourself again. Give **B** some suggestions about where he or she went wrong. Allow **B** to paraphrase your remarks a second time. If correct, move on. If not, try to explain yourself again. Repeat as many times as necessary. Do **NOT** move on until you feel that **B** has understood you perfectly.

Person B: Respond to **A**'s original statement. When you do, limit yourself to a single thought, idea or feeling. Keep it to one sentence.

Person A: Paraphrase. Translate what you've heard into your own words. Try as hard as you can to understand exactly what **B** has said.

Person B: Indicate whether or not **A**'s paraphrase was correct. If **A** has understood you, say "Yes, that's right" and move on to the next step. If **A** has not understood you, say "No, that's not it" and try to express yourself again. Give **A** some suggestions about where he or she went wrong. Allow **A** to paraphrase your remarks a second time. If correct, move on. If not, try to explain yourself again. Repeat as many times as necessary. Do **NOT** move on until you feel that **A** has understood you perfectly.

Person A: Respond to **B**'s remark. (Go to the top of the exercise and repeat.)

Don't ask questions when you paraphrase. Just try to restate the other person's words to the best of your ability. It's easy to get sidetracked by asking questions like "What do you mean when you say_____

_____?"

Once you do this, you throw away the format of this exercise and may find it impossible to return to it. Then the argument might spiral out of control. If you don't think you've understood the other person perfectly, just paraphrase as much as you do understand. Remember, the other person will get the chance to explain himself/herself a second time, if necessary. Conversation will not advance until you both understand each other perfectly. For handy reference, here's a very brief summary of how this exercise works:

Paraphrasing Rule Summary

Person **A**:   Make a statement expressing a single thought.

Person **B**:   Paraphrase.

Person **A**:   Say whether or not **B**'s paraphrase was correct. If so, move on. If not, repeat.

Person **B**:   Respond to **A**'s original statement by expressing a single thought.

Person **A**:   Paraphrase.

Person **B**:   Say whether or not **A**'s paraphrase was correct. If so, move on. If not, repeat.

Person **A**:   Make a statement.

And so on.

Practice this exercise with family or friends at least once a week for a half hour to an hour. When you practice, choose a mildly controversial topic for discussion. If you discuss something uncontroversial like the weather, the exercise will seem pointless and won't go very far. These rehearsals will prepare you to use the technique correctly when you are truly angry and need it to address a real topic.

Now that you understand how the process works in simple communication, let's look at how this technique can help you resolve difficult issues:

Paraphrasing Example

A: I feel angry.

B: You are feeling angry right now.

A: Yeah.

B: The tone of your voice just then was a little sharp and it made me feel attacked.

A: Okay, so you felt attacked because I snapped at you when I said "Yeah."

B: That's correct.

A: Sorry. I'm snapping at you because it seems like I'm the only one who does any chores around here.

B: You're angry because you feel I don't help out with the chores.

A: That's it. That's what I'm feeling.

B: I always mean to help out, but I forget.

A: You forget to do chores, but you *would* help me if you could remember.

B: Yeah.

A: Then we need to help your memory.

B: You're saying that I have a problem because of my memory.

A: Well, no, not exactly. I'm just saying that your memory is a problem in this instance.

B: Oh, so you mean that, when it comes to this situation, my memory is a problem.

A: Now you've got it.

B: Well, I'd find it helpful if we could assign a regular schedule for chores.

A: You'd remember if you knew exactly when you were supposed to do chores.

B: Yeah.

A: Okay, let's divide things so that I do everything one day and you do everything the next.

B: You want to alternate doing the chores every day.

A: Exactly.

B: I've got a better idea. I'll set the table every night and you'll clean up.

A: You want to set the table all the time and have me clean up all the time.

B: Right.

A: But I hate cleaning up.

B: You don't like cleaning up.

A: No way.

B: I don't like it, either.

A: You hate cleaning up, too.

B: That's right.

A: This is no good. One of us has to clean up.

B: You're saying that neither of us wants to do the job, but one of us has to do it.

A: Yes.

B: Let's try to compromise.

A: You think we can compromise.

B: That's right.

A: Okay, let's switch off. The first week, I'll set the table and you'll clean up. Then next week, you'll set the table and I'll clean up.

B: You want us to alternate setting and cleaning every week.

A: Exactly.

B: Sounds good to me.

A: You're comfortable with that idea.

B: You got it.

A: Good, so we agree.

B: Yes, we agree.

Hopefully, this example shows you in more detail how the paraphrasing technique can help resolve your problems. Sometimes when people argue, they allow the argument to get off-track by introducing side issues that have nothing to do with the matter at hand. I call this "kitchen sinking," because people throw everything into the discussion except the kitchen sink. The wonderful thing about paraphrasing is that it keeps the discussion on one track. It stops people from introducing pet peeves or complaints that might derail the argument. Ask your friends and family to read this portion of the book. Then ask them to practice paraphrasing with you. Have them agree to use the technique whenever an argument is about to start.

In addition, I also recommend that you and your family hold a family conference once a week for at least an hour. Have everyone participate. Hold it in a special place like the dining room, where everyone can gather together around the table. Use this time to bring up issues and discuss them together. Allow everyone in the family to speak (if people can't talk without yelling at one another, introduce the floor exercise). Discuss what is going well in the family or what is going badly. By holding regular family meetings, you can often head off problems before they develop—this is what we call "preventative maintenance." Don't spend all of your family time focused on the negative. Bring up the positive as well and spend time doing something fun together. This can bring back good feelings toward one another that your family might have otherwise lost.

Teen Anger Exercise

Think of a relationship in your life that needs improving. In the space which follows, write down three changes you would like the other person to make in order to improve the relationship. For instance, you might write *I would like him to stop drinking* or *I want her to pay attention to me*. Then write three things you need to change about yourself in order to improve the relationship. For example, you might write *I need to con-*

trol my temper or *I need to consider her thoughts as well as my own.* If you like, you can ask the other person to make up a similar list for him/herself. Please remember, though, that ultimately you can only control the things that *you* do. If the other person chooses not to participate, don't worry about it. Take control of yourself and make the changes that *you* need to make.

Three things I would like _____ (fill in person's name) **to do to improve our relationship:**

1) _____

_____

_____

2) _____

_____

_____

3) _____

_____

_____

Three things I need to do to improve our relationship:

1) _____

_____

_____

2) _____

_____

_____

3) _____

_____

_____

If the other person chooses to participate in this exercise, have him write down what he would like you to do to improve the relationship and what he can do to improve it in the space that follows.

Three things I would like _____ (fill in person's name) **to do to improve our relationship:**

1) _____

_____

_____

2) _____

_____

_____

3) _____

_____

_____

Three things I need to do to improve our relationship:

1) _____

_____

_____

2) _____

_____

_____

3) _____

_____

_____

If another person has completed this exercise with you, then sit down and read your lists to each other. Commit to the changes that you both need to make. If only you completed this exercise, then go to the other person with whom you are having problems and read her your list. Let that person know that you are committed to improving your relationship. By sharing this information with the other person, you help rebuild the relationship. **Paste your list to your bathroom mirror, inside your locker or in some other prominent place so that you will see it often and are reminded of your commitment to change.**

Teen Anger Listening Skills

"I know that you believe you understand what you think I said,
But I'm not sure you realize that what you heard is not what I meant."

We Communicate...
  ...not by what we are, but by what listeners understand.

We Communicate...
  ...not by what we intend to say, but by what listeners see, hear and
  are willing to accept.

We Communicate...
  ...not by what we say, but by what listeners hear.

Focus on the other person when you are communicating. Always take the time to see that he or she is getting your message. Your efforts will be well worth it when your communications become more effective, understanding increases and your relationships improve.

Teen Anger Tips

- When you communicate, there are many moments when your original message may be lost or distorted.
- Don't argue over who is "right" and who is "wrong"— focus on solving the problem.
- Address one issue at a time.
- Anger can often be used to conceal a deeper emotion such as sorrow or hurt.
- When you become angry, look to see if your anger is masking a deeper emotion. Get in touch with your true feelings and risk expressing them.
- When someone gets angry with you, see if you can help that person get in touch with his/her deeper feelings.
- Use and practice the Floor Exercise.
- Use and practice Paraphrasing.
- Avoid "kitchen sinking."
- Hold regular meetings with your family and spend quality time together.
- If you have a troubled relationship with someone, make a list of three things you can do to improve the situation and begin doing them.

chapter 12

Don't Trust Anyone Over the Age of Twenty-five Part II: Negotiating with the Enemy

Fall back on me, and I'll be the strength I need,
to save me now, just come face to face with me.
- Trust Company, "Downfall"

So far in this book, we've gone over several different examples of people communicating in which one person understands another person's needs and tries to meet them. However, not all attempts at communication are of this type. Often when people argue, they refuse to budge from their original positions. When no one wants to give in, we call this "reaching an impasse." I've had people say to me, "Okay, Doc, we've used all your communication skills, but the best we can do is understand why we disagree. What do we do now?" Well, the next thing is to recognize that you've still achieved something important, even though it might not seem that way. Although you haven't yet solved your problem, you *have* clarified the issue at hand. This is important, because it fosters understanding and empathy between you and the other person, which helps reduce future conflict. More significantly, it allows you to move on to the next step of conflict resolution: negotiation. Negotiation is the subject of this chapter.

Please make sure your family reads this. Since we'll be discussing negotiation, the people with whom you'll be negotiating need to learn the same skills and ground rules as you. Your entire family needs to work together on bettering their negotiation skills.

Let's look at how families can negotiate their way out of an impasse. A client of mine named Katie was fifteen when she, her mother and grandmother came to see me (Katie's dad was out of the picture). Katie's mom had manic-depressive disorder and was a recovering drug addict. The two problems made Katie's life hell. When on narcotics, Katie's mom would stop using the medication that helped her disorder. Then she would lose touch with reality and often would have to be hospitalized. When her mother was away, Katie stayed with her grandmother, a nurse in a pediatrician's office. The whole family came to see me after Katie's mom had returned from another stay in the hospital. Things at home were spiraling out of control. Unlike times past, Katie was now old enough to assert herself. She had become rebellious and disruptive, both at home and at school. Katie's mom and grandmother no longer felt they could control her.

Our sessions together clarified why Katie behaved as she did. Though there was more than one reason, the most important was that Katie didn't respect her mother. She was angry, because her mother had never properly assumed her parental role. When they interacted, the two of them seemed more like feuding sisters than they did mother and daughter. Despite everything that had happened before, I thought Katie's mom still had the potential to be a great mother. She was now off narcotics and back on the medications that kept her stable. I believed Katie's mom could become an important force in her daughter's life.

For her part, Katie's grandmother was overwhelmed by the dual pressures of work and dealing with a rebellious teenager. Her patience had worn so thin that she often felt she was on the verge of exploding. She tended to be very inconsistent in how she disciplined her granddaughter. When the grandmother was feeling calm, she gave Katie too much freedom. When she was feeling angry, she gave Katie too little freedom. During these angry moments, she would ground Katie for months at a time. Perhaps some of you are familiar with three-month groundings. As often happens in such cases, Katie's grandmother would forget about the grounding a few days after her anger had cooled. By not following through, she lost the ability to discipline Katie effectively.

Neither Katie's mom nor her grandmother thought the other knew how to raise Katie. The grandmother thought that the mother was unstable and untrustworthy; the mother thought the grandmother was out of touch and ineffective. The two of them frequently argued over these issues in front of Katie, thus undermining each other's authority in Katie's eyes. To make matters worse, Katie often played them off against each other. By instigating fights between them, Katie could fade into the background and thus get out of being in trouble.

In our talks we clarified much of what was going on in this troubled family. Our sessions helped Katie's mother and grandmother understand each other better. Once the air was cleared, the family could start solving its problems by negotiating key issues and making contracts over future behavior.

The first contract we drew up was an agreement between Katie's mom and grandmother that neither would undermine the other in front of Katie. This allowed the two of them to present a united front. The second contract was a bit more difficult to manage. It was clear to me that since Katie's grandmother was so overwhelmed by the job, Katie's mother needed to assume primary responsibility for taking care of Katie. I felt that Katie's mom was ready for the job now—but how could we convince Katie's grandmother of that? This was when we began to negotiate. Katie's grandmother agreed to back off and let Katie's mom handle things, but only so long as Katie's mom stayed on her medication and off narcotics. Both sides gave up something, but also got something in return. This is the essence of negotiation.

Once Katie's mom assumed primary responsibility for her daughter, the two of them were able to negotiate new rules on such things as curfews, dress codes, dating and so on. If Katie could prove to her mother that she could act responsibly, then her mom promised she would give her more freedom. This is a basic issue facing all teens and their parents—how to balance freedom and responsibility. If this is an issue for you and your parents, you might want to resolve it the way that Katie and her mom did: by negotiating a contract. Assume more responsibility and accept more freedom. Give up something to get something. This chapter will suggest ways to do exactly that.

The essence of negotiation lies in a problem-solving technique called "brainstorming." This is how you brainstorm:

1. State the problem or conflict as clearly as possible.
2. Ask everyone involved to write down as many solutions or alternatives that he/she can think of. Don't censor yourself by discarding answers that don't seem 'right'—just let your mind roam free and write down anything you can think of, no matter how outlandish or crazy.
3. Discuss each possible solution calmly and fairly as a group. Detail the pros and cons of each proposal. Come to an agreement on the fairest solution to the problem.

To help illustrate this procedure, let's imagine that you want to stay out late on a Saturday night but your parents won't let you. Step one of this procedure is to define the problem clearly: you think that you are mature enough to stay out late, but your parents disagree. Step two is to think up as many solutions as you can think of. Here are some possibilities:

- I can stay out as late as I want.
- I can't go out at all.
- I can stay out one hour later than usual, so long as I call home from where I am.

Step three asks you to discuss and evaluate each possible solution with your parents. Everyone would probably agree that the first and second solutions are too extreme, but the third solution represents a fair compromise. This easy and straightforward example is here to help illustrate the technique. Not all negotiations will be this easy, but the essential procedure will remain the same.

Teen Anger Exercise

Practice brainstorming. Write down a problem or conflict you've had recently with your family:

_____

_____

_____

_____

_____

Now sit down with your family and ask everyone to brainstorm for possible solutions to this problem. Using the space that follows, write down as many different solutions as you can think of—not just the solutions that you'd prefer. Write down *anything* that comes into your mind. Ask your family members to write down their solutions on separate sheets of paper.

Possible Solutions:

1) _____

_____

_____

2) _____

_____

_____

3) _____

_____

_____

4) _____

_____

_____

5) _____

_____

_____

Now have each family member read his or her solutions to the group. Then have the family discuss the pros and cons of each solution. Write them down. Use the space below to write down the pros and cons of your solutions; use separate paper to write down the pros and cons of your family members' suggested solutions.

PROS	**CONS**
1) _____	1) _____
_____	_____
_____	_____
2) _____	2) _____
_____	_____
_____	_____
3) _____	3) _____
_____	_____
_____	_____
4) _____	4) _____
_____	_____
_____	_____
5) _____	5) _____
_____	_____
_____	_____

Which solution does your family agree is the fairest? Write it down here:

_____

_____

_____

_____

The purpose of negotiation is to find a compromise to which everyone can agree. Once you find that compromise, you can write it down in a contract that each party should sign and agree to follow. This allows you to clarify what the terms of the agreement are and what each party is obligated to do.

There are two basic types of contracts. The first kind of contract is called *quid pro quo*—this is a Latin phrase that means "something for something." This kind of contract promises that one thing will be exchanged for another. I will do something for you, so long as you do something for me: "Mom, I'll wash your car tomorrow if you let me use it tonight." The second kind of contract is a compromise, in which two sides move away from their original positions to meet somewhere in the middle. In the story I told you about Katie, we saw that Katie's mom agreed to stay off drugs, while Katie's grandmother agreed to give up parental control. Both sides gave up something in order to get something. They both moved away from extreme positions to meet each other halfway. Compromise will leave some desires frustrated in order to satisfy others. If one side had all its desires satisfied while the other had all its desires frustrated, then the frustrated side would grow resentful. This is an unhealthy situation. It is much healthier to balance frustration and satisfaction when you work out a compromise.

What are the issues in your life that cause conflict and might be resolved with a contract? If you are like most teens, you probably argue with your parents over some, or perhaps all, of the following:

- ◆ Curfews
- ◆ Independence
- ◆ Parental Authority
- ◆ School Performance
- ◆ Choice of Friends, Boyfriends or Girlfriends
- ◆ Use of leisure time

The following exercise is designed to help you resolve all of these conflicts.

Teen Anger Exercise

In the space provided, describe any conflict you've had with your parents in each of the areas noted. If appropriate, write down more than one conflict next to each heading.

Curfews _____

_____

_____

_____

_____

Independence _____

_____

_____

_____

Parental Authority _____

_____

_____

_____

School Performance_____

_____

_____

_____

Choice of Friends/Boyfriends/Girlfriends_____

_____

_____

_____

Use of Leisure Time _____

_____

_____

_____

Now that you've described the conflict, use the space which follows to write down any informal contracts you may already have to address these conflicts. For example, next to "School Performance," you might write "My dad promised me $10 for every 'A' on my report card." If you don't have an informal contract to deal with a particular conflict, just leave the space blank. We will deal with those cases later.

Informal Contracts

Curfews _____

_____

_____

_____

_____

Independence _____

_____

_____

_____

_____

Parental Authority _____

_____

_____

_____

_____

School Performance_____

_____

_____

_____

_____

Choice of Friends/Boyfriends/Girlfriends_____

_____

_____

_____

_____

Use of Leisure Time _____

_____

_____

_____

_____

   Now that you've written down your informal contracts, draw up formal contracts for any conflict you still haven't resolved. The pages that follow will help you brainstorm for ideas and draw up contracts to settle your disputes. Before you start, you may want to photocopy these pages so that you have extra blanks to use in the future if other conflicts arise.

   For each of your unresolved conflicts, use the space provided to brainstorm some possible solutions. You may either do this alone or with your parents. After each solution, circle the letter 'Q' if the solution is a *quid pro quo* and circle the letter 'C' if it is a compromise. Then sit down with your parents and discuss which is the fairest solution.

Unresolved Conflicts: Brainstorming

1) Curfews   Possible solutions:

_____   Q   C

_____   Q   C

_____   Q   C

_____   Q   C

_____   Q   C

2) Independence   Possible solutions:

_____   Q   C

_____   Q   C

_____   Q   C

_____   Q   C

_____   Q   C

3) Parental Authority   Possible solutions:

_____   Q   C

_____   Q   C

_____   Q   C

_____   Q   C

_____   Q   C

4) School Performance   Possible solutions:

_____   Q   C
_____   Q   C
_____   Q   C
_____   Q   C
_____   Q   C

5) Choice of Friends/Dates   Possible solutions:

_____   Q   C
_____   Q   C
_____   Q   C
_____   Q   C
_____   Q   C

6) Use of Leisure Time   Possible solutions:

_____   Q   C
_____   Q   C
_____   Q   C
_____   Q   C
_____   Q   C

Have you and your parents agreed on the solution which is the fairest for each problem? If so, then use the following page to formally write out the contract. Again, you may want to photocopy the blank contract before writing on it so that you can use it again.

First, indicate whether the contract is a *quid pro quo* or a compromise. Then write out all the terms of the contract. Be as specific as possible. What does each party agree to do? What does each party agree to give up? When all parties have read the contract and understood it, have each sign it. Remember, only sign the contract when you feel confident you are getting that for which you asked and you are certain you can abide by the rules and conditions. Never sign a contract unless you truly commit yourself to living up to your end of the bargain.

As the weeks pass, refer back to the contract to make sure each party lives up to his/her end of the bargain. If this contract doesn't work out, you may need to negotiate a new contract.

CONTRACT

Quid Pro Quo:_____   **Compromise:** _____

_____

_____

_____

_____

_____

_____

_____

_____

_____

_____

_____

_____

_____

_____

_____

_____

_____

_____

_____

_____

Signed: _____

Signed: _____

Signed: _____

That's all there is to it! If you are ever discussing a problem and reach an impasse, use these negotiating skills to resolve the problem. Then, work out a contract to which everyone can agree. Finally, live up to your end of the bargain.

Teen Anger Tips

- Open communication will clarify what the conflict is about.
- When you discuss a problem and reach an impasse, start negotiating toward a solution.
- When you negotiate, you brainstorm for possible solutions, discuss each solution individually and then pick the fairest solution.
- Formal contracts are often necessary in relationships.
- There are two types of contracts: the *quid pro quo* and the compromise.
- In a successful contract, no one will get *everything* that he/she wants.
- You must give up something to get something.
- Take the time to write down your contracts formally and have each person involved sign it.
- Don't agree to a contract just to get someone off your back. Only agree to contracts that you truly can accept.

chapter 13

"My Name is Neo": Standing Up for Yourself

> _My suggestion is to keep your distance,_
> _Cuz right now I'm dangerous._
> - Limp Bizkit, "Break Stuff"

One of my favorite illustrations of true assertiveness comes from the popular movie _The Matrix_. In the film, the "Matrix" is a virtual-reality computer program that exists to keep humans under control. Agents are used to protect the Matrix and work to ensure that all humans submit to it. The hero, a man named Neo, has escaped from the Matrix and will one day help the rest of humanity to do the same. In a final showdown between an agent and Neo, the agent uses Neo's Matrix-given name saying menacingly, "I'm going to enjoy watching you die, Mr. Anderson." The beaten-up but unwilling to surrender hero responds strongly, "My name is Neo."

Notice the difference between the two lines of dialogue quoted from the movie. In the first line, the agent is being very aggressive and hostile. In the second, Neo is not being aggressive, nor is he being hostile. He is simply being assertive. He stands up for himself, but he does it in a non-threatening way. The difference between these two modes of expression will be the main focus of this chapter.

The best way to understand assertiveness is to picture it as being the mid-point between two extremes. One extreme is aggression: forcing your will on others through violent behavior. The other extreme is passivity:

submitting to the will of another without fighting back. Neither of these two extremes represents a healthy form of behavior. Aggressive people hurt others, and, if they suffer from guilt or remorse after they act, they also hurt themselves. At the other extreme, passive people get hurt, because they are unable to protect themselves from other people's aggression. Also, because passive people often cannot express their anger, they internalize and direct that anger against themselves, thus injuring themselves further. You should avoid these two extremes by finding a mid-point between them. This mid-point is assertiveness: standing up for yourself without being aggressive and without backing down.

Aggression - - - - - - - - - Assertiveness - - - - - - - - - - Passivity

In order to better understand what assertiveness is, we should look more closely at the two extremes of aggression and passivity. Aggression is easy to understand. Remember my two patients Tony and James? They were two people who acted out in aggressive and destructive ways. However, passivity may not be so easy to understand. In order to help you see more clearly how passive behavior can have destructive consequences in your life, I want to introduce you to Stacy, who I met in my practice.

Stacy came to see me when she was eighteen, because she was depressed and having panic attacks. During her childhood, Stacy's father had emotionally abused both her and her mother. Stacy's mom suffered from depression and panic attacks as well, and decided to divorce her husband when Stacy was just fifteen. Often victims of abuse like Stacy and her mother learn to become "people-pleasers." They attempt to stave off the abuse by keeping the abuser satisfied and content. But this is never enough for the abuser. The abuse continues anyway and the victim comes to feel helpless and trapped. Often the abuser will brainwash the victim into thinking that he/she is worthless and no good. This is what happened to Stacy. She became a people-pleaser who always sought the approval of others—her father, mother, sister, friends and boyfriends. Sometimes other people took advantage of her trusting nature. All this made Stacy angry, but she always suppressed her anger, because she was afraid to express it. She feared that releasing her anger would invite more abuse from her father.

In chapter 10, I described depression as anger turned against the self. Unexpressed anger can also manifest itself as panic or anxiety. All of that angry energy has to come out in *some* way and sometimes it comes out as anxiety or fear. This is what happened to Stacy.

During our sessions, I helped Stacy understand that anger was the root cause of her depression and anxiety. She acknowledged her anger. She made changes by becoming independent of her parents. She broke up with a boyfriend who took advantage of her and cheated on her. She stopped thinking of herself as a "caretaker" who had to assume responsibility for other people's problems. Slowly but surely, her symptoms improved. Stacy entered college and excelled in her studies. She worked full-time as a pharmacy technician in order to pay her way through school and thus not rely on her family for financial support. Next, Stacy moved out of her mom's house and into the college dormitory to further her independence.

Stacy was able to change the way she dealt with her anger. Before she came to see me, she didn't even allow herself to acknowledge she *had* any anger. But our work together helped Stacy get in touch with her true feelings. At first, she directed her anger at her mother, a "safe" target. Fortunately, Stacy's mom also had been through therapy and had learned to assert herself. She was no longer going to be anybody's victim. She did not attack Stacy in return, but she did stand up to Stacy's misplaced anger. She showed her daughter that she understood her feelings and then talked about her own experiences and anger. Rather than strike back or lie down and take it, Stacy's mom now asserted her own feelings and set limits for Stacy's angry behavior. Before therapy, Stacy's mother had been a model for how to be a victim. After therapy, Stacy's mother became a model for how to assert oneself.

Stacy followed her mother's lead by becoming less aggressive and more assertive. Like her mom, she learned to express her feelings in words. Stacy had traveled from one extreme (passivity) to another (aggressiveness) before finally finding a middle course (assertiveness). Victims of abuse often experience this kind of pendulum swing when they go through therapy.

You can learn to assert yourself positively just like Stacy did. Remember that your ultimate goal is to be able to express your angry feelings calmly and in words, not through aggressive attacks. If others hear you express yourself clearly and calmly, they will be more likely to attend to your feelings and meet your needs. This won't happen if the other person is defensive or feels the need to respond to your attack. You want to show the other person that you are stable and calm. When you feel empowered in this way, you won't need to exert control over the people in your life. You can sidestep all those petty power struggles that complicate arguments. Your ego and self-esteem will no longer be at stake. The only important thing will be resolving the conflict effectively. Remember that self-esteem does not come from your relationships with others, it comes from within yourself.

Teen Self Image Exercise

Since low self-esteem can complicate anger problems, it's important to improve one's self-image. Toward that end, I would like you to complete the following exercise. Write down some of the negative thoughts you've had about yourself. Then contradict each thought by writing down a positive statement about yourself directly under it.

Example   Negative Thought: *I'm so stupid. I would do a lot better in school if I wasn't so dumb.*

Positive Thought: *I understand things quickly when I'm interested in the subject.*

In chapter 10, we talked about rational and irrational thoughts. In this exercise, replace any irrational thoughts you may have about yourself with rational ones. As we've said before, beware of thoughts that dictate what you "should," "ought" or "must" be or do. Change these thoughts to preferences. Doing this will keep you from destructively condemning yourself if you fail to meet this obligation. Expressing preferences leaves you room for tolerance and allows you to forgive yourself.

Example   Negative Thought: *I should be more patient with my little brother.*

Positive Thought: *It would be better if I were more patient with my little brother.*

1) Negative Thought _____

_____

Positive Thought _____

_____

2) Negative Thought _____

_____

Positive Thought _____

_____

3) Negative Thought _____

Positive Thought _____

_____

4) Negative Thought _____

Positive Thought _____

_____

5) Negative Thought _____

Positive Thought _____

_____

Recognizing Anger Exercise

An important step in managing your anger is learning to recognize the physical sensations that lead up to an anger attack. Different emotions will cause your body to react in different ways and these ways will vary from person to person. Below you will see a list of various different emotions. In the space across from each, write down how your body reacts when you feel that emotion. For example, across from "Irritated," you might write "I frown" or "I clench my fists." Across from "Mad," you might write "my muscles feel tense" or "my heart starts beating quickly." Use this information to help clue yourself in when you're about to get angry.

Emotion	Physical Sensations
Irritated	_____
Annoyed	_____
Frustrated	_____
Mad	_____
Pissed Off	_____
Enraged	_____
Furious	_____

Explosive   _____

Nervous   _____

Anxious   _____

Panicky   _____

Frightened   _____

Terrified   _____

Blue   _____

Sad   _____

Despair   _____

Amused   _____

Happy   _____

Joyous   _____

Many teens as well as adults have difficulty getting in touch with their emotions. This is an underlying problem in assertiveness. How can you express how you feel if you don't *know* how you feel? Sometimes people in this situation grow resentful because they think others *should* be able to read their minds and understand their feelings. This is irrational thinking. Never assume that others *should* know how you feel—it's your responsibility to tell them.

Feelings are a part of being human. There's nothing you can feel that someone else hasn't felt at some point in human history. We all have the ability to feel and we all feel similar things. Therefore, feelings are an excellent bridge to help connect with other people. When you can explain to others how you feel, they will be better able to respond to you more appropriately.

People are not always honest and open about their emotions. Sometimes we have emotions we think are unpleasant and unwelcome—emotions like hate, fear, anger, jealousy and so on. Because we don't want others to see these negative emotions (or because we don't want to see them in ourselves), we learn to hide them. We suppress them, shove them aside, tuck them out of sight or otherwise ignore them. We act as though they are not even there. Sometimes we try to cover this up by pretending to feel positive emotions that we don't really feel! Pretending to feel happy when we really aren't is just another form of hiding. In order for you to manage your anger effectively, you are going to have to be truthful when expressing how you feel. This exercise will help you do just that.

Teen Emotion Exercise

In the left column that follows, write down emotions that you dislike feeling. In the right column, write down emotions that you enjoy feeling.

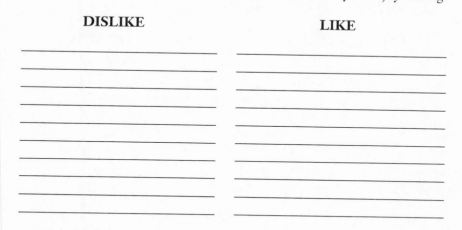

DISLIKE	LIKE

Now read over the emotions you listed in the left column. Have you ever felt these emotions but hid them from other people or from yourself? How did you do that? Why did you do that? Read over the emotions you listed in the right column. Have you ever pretended to feel these emotions when you really didn't feel them? How did you do that? Why did you do that?

It's difficult enough to cope with these kinds of hidden emotions; we also have to deal with the fact that society has placed moralistic judgments on certain kinds of feelings. We are taught to think that it's "bad" to feel one way and "good" to feel another. So we strive never to have the "bad" feelings and only have the "good" ones. This never works, of course. "Bad" feelings like anger or hate come upon us despite our wishes and then we feel guilty for having them. We begin to see ourselves as "bad" people who don't deserve approval; we despise ourselves and expect the same reaction from others. No wonder some people find it easier to pretend they don't have those "bad" feelings. On the other hand, there are certain "good" feelings that people think they are obligated to feel. Society approves of these "good" feelings, so even when we don't feel these ways, sometimes we pretend to feel them in order to gain the approval of others. Realistically, no feeling is either bad *or* good. Feelings simply *are*.

Good Feeling/Bad Feeling Exercise

Have you learned to think of certain feelings as "bad?" Write them down in the left column below. Have you learned to think of certain feelings as "good?" Write them down in the right column.

"BAD" FEELINGS	"GOOD" FEELINGS

You will find it so much easier to deal with your feelings (and the feelings of others) if you simply accept them as they are and throw away labels like "good" and "bad." It's hard enough for us to express our emotions as it is. We find it easy to discuss ideas, intellectualize, analyze problems and express opinions, but we find it hard to open up and simply say how we feel. Rather than risk getting hurt, we build defenses to protect and hide our feelings. Sometimes those defenses become so strong that our feelings become inaccessible even to ourselves. If you keep a large part of yourself hidden from view, you will never know yourself, nor will anyone else ever come to know you. Your relationship with others will always be guarded, defensive, wary, cautious and distant. Who wants to live that way?

Feelings exist in the here and now. Whenever we interact with others, we always respond on an emotional level. Therefore, emotion can be the bridge that allows us to connect and communicate with other people. Talking about emotions allows us to talk about experiences we all share in common. Thus, the more skills you have for dealing with your feelings, the more effectively you will be able to communicate and relate to others.

How Teens Should Handle Feelings

1. Remember that having feelings is a basic part of being human.
2. Know that there are a small number of feelings that underline much of human experience.

3. Acknowledge that feelings are neither "good" nor "bad"; they simply *are*.
4. Realize you can't make feelings go away by ignoring or suppressing them.
5. Believe that suppressed feelings will simply rise up in another form unless you acknowledge that they exist.
6. Expressing your feelings directly can result in clear, meaningful communication.
7. Stating your feelings directly will often solve problems.
8. Feelings that you refuse to acknowledge will only reappear as unproductive thoughts and behaviors.
9. Release yourself from painful feelings by working through them.
10. Feelings you refuse to recognize can eventually dominate your entire life.

Learn to recognize your feelings at the very moment you have them. Don't push your feelings away—learn to let them be just as they are. When you feel scared, admit to yourself, "I'm scared." When you feel angry, say "I'm angry." Your emotions are part of who you are, so know them and express them honestly.

The next chart will list various emotions and the thoughts that may have led up to them to help you become more aware of your feelings.

Emotion and Thoughts Chart

Emotion	Thoughts That Lead to This Emotion
Sadness or depression	Loss: romantic rejection, death of a loved one, losing a job or the failure to achieve an important personal goal.
Guilt or shame	You believe that you've hurt someone or that you've failed to live up to certain standards. You feel guilt when you judge yourself; you feel shame when you feel judged by others.
Anger, annoyance, irritation or resentment	You feel that someone is treating you unfairly or trying to take advantage of you
Frustration	You insist that things should be different when life falls short of your expectations. This can include the way

you act (*I shouldn't be making these mistakes!*), the way someone else acts (*He should be on time!*), or the way life is in general (*Why are the halls always crowded when I'm late for class?*).

Anxiety, worry, fear, nervousness or panic	You believe you are in danger, because you think something bad is about to happen: *What if the plane crashes?* or *What if my mind goes blank in speech class?*
Inferiority or inadequacy	You compare yourself to others and conclude that you are not as good as they are. You think you are less talented, attractive, charming, successful or intelligent: *She's so cute; all the guys are chasing her. I'm just average. There's nothing very special about me.*
Loneliness	You feel unhappy, because you are alone and feel you do not get enough love and attention from others.
Hopelessness or discouragement	You feel convinced that your problems will go on forever and that things will never improve: *I'll never get over this depression.*

Descriptions of Feelings

Here are some descriptions of some basic human emotions. Use these words when explaining to others how you feel:

Anger	Fear	Guilt
Displeased	Afraid	Remorse
Indignant	Frightened	Lonely
Exasperated	Timid	Isolated
Irritated	Alarmed	Low spirits
Annoyed	Uneasy	Dejected
Frustrated	Anxious	
Furious	Eagerness	

Shame
Embarrassed
Humiliated
Chagrined
Ashamed
Inadequate
Insufficient
Lacking
Incomplete
Dumb
Worthless
Crazy

Happy
Pleasure
Contentment
Glad
Joyous

Sad
Sorrowful
Melancholic
Mournful
Hurt
Pained

Resentful
Unresolved anger

How We Hide Feelings

We often try to hide how we feel. But when we do, we may not be aware how these defensive actions come across to others. This chart lists some common ways in which we attempt to hide our feelings and the different ways those attempts will appear to other people.

Defensive behavior: justifying, intellectualizing, rationalizing, theorizing, analyzing, generalizing.
How others can view that behavior: superior, arrogant, controlling, manipulative.
Possible hidden feelings: insecurity, uncertainty, fear of emotions

Defensive behavior: disagreeing, threatening, attacking, glaring, making sarcastic comments.
How others can view that behavior: stubborn, defiant, hostile, obnoxious.
Possible hidden feelings: anger, sorrow, fear, shame, hurt.

Defensive behavior: agreeing, flattering, joking, smiling, apologizing.
How others can view that behavior: "people-pleasing," wishy-washy, phony, weak.
Possible hidden feelings: fear, anger, loneliness, shame.

Defensive behavior: evading, withdrawing, running away, minimizing, changing the subject, staying silent.
How others can view that behavior: aloof, indifferent, sullen, suspicious, rejecting.
Possible hidden feelings: fear, anger, insecurity, hurt.

Defensive behavior: criticizing, moralizing, rationalizing, projecting, judging, justifying.
How others can view that behavior: angry, resentful, intolerant, self-pitying, "holier-than-thou."
Possible hidden feelings: insecurity, anger, fear.

We've discussed that it is often hard for people to get in touch with their feelings. When asked how they feel about something, people often answer by saying something like "I feel as though he lectures me" or "I feel like she is not listening to me." However, these statements don't really answer the question, because they express *thoughts*, not *feelings*. There are only four basic feelings: mad, sad, scared and glad. When you discuss your feelings, use one of these four words (or variations of them) only when describing how you feel. Let's rephrase the two examples listed above so they correspond to this rule. We should say **"I'm mad** about the fact that he lectures me" and **"I'm sad** that she won't listen to me." Focus on saying what you *feel*, not what you *think*. After you've correctly stated your feelings, then follow up by expressing your preference about how you'd like the situation to be different. In the first example, you might add: "I'd prefer to have a conversation with him and not just listen to him talk." In the second example, you might add: "I'd like her to understand how I feel, because I care about her."

To help understand this point, imagine that your best friend has just blown you off. When asked how you feel about this, you might say "I feel that she always ignores me." However, this statement expresses a *thought*, not a *feeling*. Express yourself in terms of feelings and preference and you will better describe what you really mean:

I feel angry that she ignored me when I wanted to talk to her.

I would like her to pay attention to me when I need her help.

When you express your feelings in this manner, you are being assertive, not aggressive. You are clearly stating how you feel, but you are doing it in a non-threatening manner. This is a more effective method of communication, because it is less likely to cause the other person to be defensive and to provoke you again. The other person will be more likely to understand you and be willing to work things out.

Teen Anger Exercise

Learn to express yourself in terms of feelings and preferences by using the format which follows. Complete the statements by describing things that make you angry and how you would prefer the situation to be different.

Example   I feel angry that *my older sister won't stop picking on me.*
I would like *to be treated like someone who has feelings.*

1) I feel angry that _____

I would like _____

_____

2) I feel angry that _____

I would like _____

_____

3) I feel angry that _____

I would like _____

_____

4) I feel angry that _____

I would like _____

_____

Read silently what you have just written to yourself. Now read it out loud. If a friend is nearby, practice saying it to him or her. Use this format ("I feel angry that…I would like…") to express yourself whenever you feel angry. When you express yourself successfully, treat yourself to a pleasant activity or something you enjoy—this will reinforce your behavior and make it more likely that you will respond the same way next time. Ask others for feedback. Ask them: "How did you feel when I expressed my anger that way?" Chances are that they will be pleased you expressed yourself in such a constructive manner. Be aware, though, that not everyone may respond this way. Remember that you have no control over how others think or act. If the other person cannot appreciate the positive changes you've made, then let that go. Don't obsess over the idea that he or she "must" appreciate it or "ought to" respond positively. Ultimately, you only have control over yourself, so stay focused on **YOU**. Don't give up on this method even if a few people fail to appreciate it.

As you become more assertive, there will come times when you will have to tell others *NO*. Many people find this hard to do. They often feel compelled to do things that they really don't want to do, simply because they don't want to displease the other person. Afterwards, they resent the fact that they were "forced" to act contrary to their wishes. Sometimes people will concoct elaborate excuses to wriggle out of the obligation. Sometimes people will structure their entire lives differently just to avoid saying NO. I've heard of people who sold off their pick-up trucks, because they were sick of constantly being asked to help their friends move or haul garbage. I've even heard of people who moved to a different state to avoid relatives who were always asking favors. Isn't this crazy? How much easier their lives would be if they had simply learned to say NO! Don't repeat their mistakes. When someone asks you to do something you don't want to do, answer with a simple and pleasant "No." or "I'm sorry, but I can't." Don't explain why you are saying no—this only prolongs the conversation and makes things more difficult. Let a firm but friendly "No" suffice.

Teen Assertiveness Exercise

When you assert yourself, you express your feelings clearly and directly, without being threatening and without being passive. Sometimes this means asking for what you want, sometimes it means saying "No." Undoubtedly there are some people in your life who are easier to deal with than others. In the space that follows, rank the important people in your life. Start with those with whom you think it will be easy to assert yourself and end with those with whom you think it will be hard.

Easiest   _____

                _____

                _____

                _____

                _____

                _____

                _____

                _____

Hardest   _____

Now let's work down your list. In the next few days, I want you to approach the first person on your list and express yourself directly to him or her in the ways we've discussed in this chapter. Use clear and concrete language to state your needs and feelings. If applicable, use the "I feel angry that....I would like...." format to express yourself. If applicable, give that person a firm but friendly "no." Then, in the next few days, try the same thing with the second person on your list. A few days later, move on to the third person and so on. The more often you practice expressing yourself this way, the easier it will become. You may also find the people on your list reacting in unexpected ways. People that you thought would be difficult might prove to be quite receptive to your new way of expressing your feelings.

If you find this too difficult a task at first, try a practice round with a friend before you approach the person with whom you're having difficulties. Tell your friend about the exercise and have him/her pretend to be someone on your list. Then role-play a conversation you might have with that person. State your feelings clearly and have your friend react the way the other person would. Ask your friend to give you positive responses, not just negative ones. Don't be afraid then to go on and have these conversations for real.

Teen Anger Tips

- Assertiveness stands as the mid-point between the two extremes of aggressiveness and passivity.
- Aggressive and passive behaviors both have destructive consequences for others and for ourselves.
- Because aggressive and passive behaviors are learned, they can be unlearned.
- You can learn to assert yourself.
- You assert yourself when you express your feelings calmly and in words, rather than acting violently or saying nothing at all.
- Don't engage in petty power struggles.
- Assertion requires self-esteem. If you don't respect yourself, others won't respect you either.
- Replace negative thoughts about yourself with positive ones.
- Don't think in terms of how things "should," "ought to" or "must be." Express these thoughts as preferences.
- Often physical sensations will give you clues as to how you are feeling. Use this information to find out how you feel so that you can express yourself properly.
- When expressing what you feel, don't say what you THINK.
- Remember that there are only four basic emotions: mad, sad, scared and glad. Express your feelings using these words (or variations of them).
- Use the format "I feel angry that…. I would like…." in order to make your feelings understood.
- Don't agree to do things you'd rather not do. Simply say "No."

chapter 14

Getting High

I was gonna go to class before I got high.
I coulda cheated and I coulda passed, but I got high.
I'm taking it next semester and I know why...
Because I got high, because I got high, because I got high.
- Afroman, "Because I Got High"

Alcohol and drugs can have very harmful effects on you, your relationships and your future. James, the young man I introduced to you in chapter 1, is an example of how these substances can damage your life. James had both an anger problem and a drinking problem. In truth, the two problems were interrelated. Both his drinking and his anger were caused by his pain over his mother's alcoholism and his dad's hyper-criticism. Before his family experienced these problems, James had earned good grades at school and excelled in sports. Then his parents divorced and his family fell apart. When his parents gave up on their marriage, James began to give up on himself. He decided that there was no reason why he should do what was expected of him. He thought, *My parents didn't do the right thing, so why should I?*

James' family only began addressing their internal problems after James was repeatedly caught getting drunk at school. James' behavior was a cry for help—after all, he was simply repeating his mother's most self-destructive behavior. The most important thing to note is that James' drinking went hand-in-hand with his anger problems. One theory is that some people become alcoholics because they are genetically predisposed toward that behavior. However, another theory is that some people become alcoholics to mask pain that they cannot acknowledge. For these people, alcohol abuse and anger mismanagement are expressions of deeper underlying problems.

Some people don't even have to take alcohol or drugs themselves to have their lives dramatically influenced by substance abuse. Another client of mine named Bruce walked into his first session with me accompanied by his mother. I asked his mom why she had brought him to me, expecting to hear the same-old answer: she was forcing him to come. I was pleasantly surprised to hear her say: "I brought him because he asked me to." Wonderful! Clearly, Bruce was motivated to change.

After his mom left, Bruce opened up to me. He said he was angry over his father's lack of involvement in his life. Bruce described his dad as a free-spirit who acted more like a teenager than an adult. After divorcing his wife, Bruce's dad plunged into a life of parties, drug use and carefree flings with much younger women. Bruce wished his father would become more responsible and stop using drugs. Although Bruce's dad was well off, he never sent his child support payments, which further angered Bruce. When his father asked him to move into his house, Bruce refused. He did not want to abandon his mother and knew that his dad's lifestyle would not be good for him. Bruce was strongly opposed to using drugs.

All of this made Bruce feel angry. He took his rage out on his mom; in fact, that is why he came to me for help. Bruce felt guilty, because he was directing his anger at someone who didn't deserve it. In our sessions together, Bruce was able to release his feelings. This helped reduce his anger. Although Bruce was primarily angry due to his dad abandoning him, he also was angry about his dad's irresponsible drug use. Once again, substance abuse and anger were interrelated. Unlike James, Bruce did not abuse substances himself. However, both James and Bruce had a parent who used substances irresponsibly. In both cases, substance abuse was the cause of angry behavior. The link between anger and substance abuse will be the focus of this chapter.

There is no doubt that substance abuse has a large role to play in many forms of angry behavior. Research has shown that 65 percent of all physically abusive incidents in relationships occur when at least one of the participants is under the influence of alcohol or drugs. Some substances like alcohol, marijuana and prescription tranquilizers have what are known as "dis-inhibiting" effects. This means that they lower our natural controls, making it easier for us to lash out in anger. Other substances such as cocaine and speed can increase irritability and angry feelings.

When you go through withdrawal after taking drugs, you may also feel irritable and angry. All of this demonstrates the strong link between substance abuse and anger.

Substance abuse problems are not signs of weakness, nor are they personal flaws. There are reasons why people have these problems. Some people are genetically disposed to become addicted to alcohol or drugs—these traits are passed down from generation to generation. Some people are conditioned at an early age to view addictive behavior as normal. Indeed, the attitudes that your parents and friends have about substance use go a long way toward influencing your own. If your friends light up a joint to relax, you might do the same. If your father downs a drink to cope with stress, you might do the same. If your mother pops a pill to deal with boredom, you might do the same.

To those of you reading this book who do not use alcohol or drugs, I want to say: Great! Good for you. I'm glad that you are substance-free. But don't skip over this chapter! The things that we will discuss may still apply to you. If you have a family member who abuses substances, this may account for some of your angry behavior. Remember that James was angry, because he couldn't keep his mother from drinking. He had to learn that he had no control over his mother's problem. What was true for James may be true for you as well. If a family member's substance abuse is fueling your anger, you must learn that you cannot assume responsibility for that person's addiction. You might consider joining Al-Ateen or Nar-Ateen, two popular groups for teens who have substance abusers in their families.

Know that it is futile to try to communicate with someone when he or she is under the influence. Don't even bother trying. Alcohol and drugs affect the brain in many different ways, the most important being that they knock out our pre-frontal cortex, the area of the brain which handles reasoning. When this area of the brain is disabled, people become more likely to act out on impulse and emotion. It is impossible to have a real conversation with someone who can't reason effectively. Walk away and wait until that person is sober or straight. If you are angry, take a Time Out. Don't try to reconnect after the Time Out until the other person is no longer under the influence of a substance.

The two tests which follow will help determine if you or someone in your family has a substance abuse problem. If you think that you have a problem, I will give you advice about how to get help. If you think someone in your family has a problem, remember that you cannot change that person—he/she must decide to change on his/her own. Sometimes when people are unwilling to make this change, substance abuse professionals will stage something called an "intervention." This is a session where all the people hurt by the substance abuser's behavior confront him/her about the problem. If you feel that you need to explore this route, contact your local Al-Ateen or Nar-Ateen group for information on professional counselors who run interventions.

Teen Substance Abuse Screening Test #1

Answer each question by checking the appropriate box.

1. Do you feel you are a normal drinker or substance user? ☐ Yes ☐ No

2. Do friends or relatives think you are a normal drinker or substance user? ☐ Yes ☐ No

Give yourself 2 points for every "No" answer given to these first two questions.

3. Have you ever lost friends or girlfriends/boyfriends because of drinking or drug use? ☐ Yes ☐ No

4. Have you ever gotten into trouble because of drinking or drug use? ☐ Yes ☐ No

5. Have you ever neglected your obligations, your family or your work for two or more days in a row because of drinking or drug use? ☐ Yes ☐ No
☐ Yes ☐ No

6. Have you ever had severe shaking, heard voices or seen things that weren't there after heavy drinking or drug use? ☐ Yes ☐ No

7. Have you ever been arrested for driving while under the influence? ☐ Yes ☐ No

Add 2 points to your score for every "Yes" answer given to questions 3 through 7.

8. Have you ever gone to anyone for help about your drinking or drug use? ☐ Yes ☐ No

9. Have you ever been in a hospital because ☐ Yes ☐ No
of drinking or drug use?

10. Have you ever attended a meeting of Alcoholics ☐ Yes ☐ No
or Narcotics Anonymous (AA or NA)?

Add 5 points to your score for every "Yes" answer given to the last three questions.

If you score 3 or less points, you do not have a problem with substance abuse. If you scored 4 points, you may have a substance abuse problem. If you scored 5 or more points, then you almost certainly have a substance abuse problem and should seek help.

Teen Substance Abuse Screening Test #2

The following twelve questions have been excerpted from material appearing in the pamplet, "Is AA for You?" and has been reprinted with permission of Alcoholics Anonymous World Services, Inc. (AAWS) Permission to reprint this material does not mean that AAWS has reviewed and/or endorses this publication. AA is a program of recovery from alcoholism only--use of AA material in any non-AA context does not imply otherwise. Nevertheless, I feel that reading the questions and thinking about your answers will be helpful for you whether you use alcohol or drugs.

1. Have you ever decided to stop drinking for ☐ Yes ☐ No
a week or so, but only lasted for a couple
of days?

2. Do you wish people would mind their own ☐ Yes ☐ No
business about your drinking and stop telling
you what to do?

3. Have you ever switched from one kind of ☐ Yes ☐ No
drink to another in the hope that this would
keep you from getting drunk?

4. Have you had to have an "eye-opener" ☐ Yes ☐ No
upon awakening during the past year?

5. Do you envy people who can drink without ☐ Yes ☐ No
getting into trouble?

6. Have you had problems connected with drinking during the past year?   ☐ Yes   ☐ No

7. Has your drinking caused trouble at home?   ☐ Yes   ☐ No

8. Do you ever try to get "extra" drinks at a party because you do not get enough?   ☐ Yes   ☐ No

9. Do you tell yourself you can stop drinking anytime you want to, even though you keep keep getting drunk when you don't mean to?   ☐ Yes   ☐ No

10. Have you missed days of school or work because of drinking?   ☐ Yes   ☐ No

11. Do you have "blackouts"?   ☐ Yes   ☐ No

12. Have you ever felt that your life would be better if you did not drink?   ☐ Yes   ☐ No

What's your score?

Did you answer YES four or more times? If so, you may have serious problems with alcohol. Thousands of people who've taken this same test and answered YES four or more times have gone to AA seeking help. Though some take longer than others to take that step, they all eventually realized the truth about themselves: their drinking was causing problems in their lives and threatening their health, work, relationships and happiness. However, only *you* can decide whether you think AA is for you. Try to keep an open mind on the subject. If you are unsure, read on to learn more about AA and how it can help you.

Is AA for you?

Again, if you gave four or more YES answers, you likely have a problem with alcohol and may need to stay away from it altogether. Alcoholism is a disease from which many suffer. A great number of these people have come to the realization that they can never drink safely and so choose to stop.

AA's philosophy is based on the idea of "one day at a time." At meetings, members talk about their drinking, the problems it caused and how they are coping without alcohol each day. New members are assigned mentors to help them through the process.

Merely joining AA will not solve all your problems. However, by controlling your dependence on alcohol—and AA members appear to have much success in doing so—your life will become much more manageable.

If you have taken both written tests and are still unsure whether you have a problem, then take a third action test to be certain: give up all substance use for ninety days. If you can do it, then you don't have a problem. If you can't, then you do. It's as simple as that.

Some of you may go for long periods without using any substance and then suddenly consume a lot of alcohol or drugs in a short period of time. This is called "binging." This may be a problem in your life if you cannot abstain from using substances for at least ninety days or longer. Try abstaining for four months or six months. If you can do it, you don't have a problem. If you can't, then you do.

Some of you may have been prescribed medication by a doctor and are now using it recreationally or more frequently than prescribed. If so, you may have a prescription drug abuse problem. In this case, you cannot simply stop taking these medications, because this may have harmful side effects. Discuss this situation with your doctor. Your doctor may set up a program that slowly weans you off these medications.

The important question to ask yourself is simply this: *Does my substance use cause problems in my life?* These problems may occur at school, at work or within your relationships with family and friends. Does your family have a history of substance abuse problems? If so, you may be genetically predisposed toward substance abuse. Look over this chapter again and ask yourself honestly: *Do I have an alcohol or drug problem?* If the answer is yes, you must seek further evaluation and treatment. I will discuss how to do this later in the chapter. This is a problem you will need to address before (or, at least, along side) your anger management work.

Many substance abusers think they can solve their problem on their own without outside help. All too often, I have seen these people stop their substance abuse for a short time and then fall back into old patterns of behavior. Don't let this happen to you. If you think you have a substance abuse problem, you *must* seek help. Where to go will depend on your individual circumstances and the resources available in your area. We will discuss the options more fully in the next chapter.

If you decide to seek help, there is a wide range of treatment available. The best method of treatment will be determined by the substance in question and the type and extent of the problem. Remember that substance abuse will often lead to substance dependence. Sometimes this dependence means that your mind craves the substance as essential to your mental well-being—this is called psychological addiction. Sometimes this dependence means that your body craves that substance as well—this is called physiological addiction. Remember that any such substance is a chemical that alters your body's natural balance. Your body may grow accustomed to this foreign chemical, requiring you to use more of it to achieve the desired effect. When this happens, we say your body has developed a "tolerance" for the substance. The higher your tolerance, the more of the substance you need to take to get high. The more substance you take, the higher your tolerance becomes. As you can see, this is a dangerous cycle.

Once addicted, your body will still crave the substance when you've stopped using it. This is called "withdrawal." The symptoms of withdrawal can often be so painful that people cannot kick their abusive habit by themselves. These people require hospitalization or close medical supervision to free their bodies from the need of the drug. In some cases, people need to be put on a replacement medication in order to cope with the great pain of withdrawal. After a time, they are weaned off the replacement medication. As you can see, freeing yourself from chemical dependence is frequently not an easy thing. You will need help. In the next chapter, we will discuss how to seek that help.

Often it is not enough simply to survive through this withdrawal period—sometimes the abuser will need to stay under medical supervision for an extended period of time. This is called rehabilitation or "rehab" for short. Rehab programs usually last about a month, though some may last longer. During this time, the patient will receive continuing medical treatment to fight the addiction. He or she will also get advice on nutrition and general medical needs. In addition, the patient will receive one-on-one counseling from trained professionals as well as group counseling with other patients who are also trying to kick the habit. The focus here is to educate the patient about the harmful effects of substance abuse and help that person correct his/her destructive behavior.

When the patient is finally released from the program, the doctors will set up an outside program that will include ongoing medication, individual counseling sessions and support group sessions. When an individual continues rehab after leaving the hospital, we call this treatment "outpatient rehab." There are many different types of outpatient rehab programs—some are more demanding and restrictive than others. Choosing which outpatient rehab program is best for you will depend on the type of addiction and the extent of the problem.

One of the most important (and most commonly known) elements of these outpatient rehab programs is the twelve-step support group programs. The first of these programs to exist was Alcoholics Anonymous (AA), which was soon followed by Narcotics Anonymous (NA), a similar program for drug abusers. People who have abused both alcohol and drugs may find it very helpful to attend both groups. There are a great many other groups of this type, like Gamblers Anonymous (GA), along with groups for family members of addicts, such as Adult Children of Alcoholics (ACOA). If you are a teen who has a substance-abusing parent, you might consider joining a support group such as Al-Anon, Nar-Anon or Al-Ateen to help you deal with your parent's problem and its repercussions on you. The groups mentioned meet in towns all across the country; probably there is a chapter very near where you live. They are always free.

Alcoholics Anonymous and Narcotics Anonymous have helped millions of people to stay clean and sober. However, new participants must do more than just go to meetings—they must also choose a sponsor to guide them through the steps of recovery. You will find that these sponsors will give support and comfort along this difficult journey. Other members will often offer support as well, passing along their phone numbers and asking the newcomer to call at anytime. New members should make use of this support and call whenever they feel the urge to abuse substances. The older members will talk them through it until they can regain control.

Some of my teen clients have told me up front that AA or NA is not for them, even before attending a meeting. I tell them to give one of these groups a try anyway. If you have a substance problem, you should give one (or both) of these programs a try, too. Commit yourself to attend for a good amount of time. These programs recommend the newcomer attend once a day for ninety days. You also might try attending different meetings in order to find a group you particularly like. Some groups are all-male, some are all-female, some are mixed, some allow smoking, some don't—there are many different groups for many different kinds of people. Find the one that's best for you.

When choosing which treatment program to follow, don't feel that you must make the decision by yourself. During your evaluation, a trained professional will recommend the course of treatment that he/she thinks is best for you. This is never something you ought to do on your own—caring specialists will be there to help you every step of the way.

Teen Anger Assignment

If you have even the slightest suspicion that you may have a substance abuse problem, tell a responsible adult. If you can not tell one of your parents, a teacher, pastor, coach or guidance counselor might be a good source of help. Make an appointment with a professional who specializes in substance abuse and keep that appointment. Do this now. Do not continue reading until you've taken this imperative step.

Even if you don't *abuse* alcohol or drugs, you might still have anger problems when you *use* them. In the future, be very careful with your anger if you are under the influence of substances. All the skills I've described here are self-control skills. Since alcohol and drugs weaken your ability to control yourself, they will increase the chance that you will throw away our anger management skills and revert to old forms of behavior. If you do relapse in this way, don't think you've moved back to square one and lost everything. You have not lost all you have gained. Recommit and start over. Give yourself a new chance. When you make great changes in your life, you may often take a step backward for every few that you take forward. As long as you stay committed, your continued course will be successful. Don't put all your energy into feeling guilty or blaming yourself for a backward step. This serves no purpose. Use this energy to get moving forward again.

You may notice you relapse into angry behavior when you drink or take drugs. This is an important signal of danger. You need to stop using the substance. It definitely has become a problem in your life. If you don't solve this problem, you stand to lose everything you've gained so far. Which is worth more to you: having healthy relationships or having an occasional drink? Planning for a future career or slipping away to smoke a joint? Don't choose the wrong path. The risk of loss is often a great tool to motivate people to give up alcohol or drugs. Every time you drink or take drugs, think of what this may cost you in the larger scheme of your life and future.

Many people with addictions do not give them up until they've "hit bottom." What it means to "hit bottom" is different for different people. Some people have to lose almost everything before they finally stop abusing substances. Some people never hit bottom and never stop. These are the people who lose their lives to their addiction. Years ago I ran an Alcohol Counseling Unit for the New York City Police Department.

One day I was introduced to Gail, a woman who had been with the Department for over thirty years and was in "end-stage alcoholism." This means that Gail was close to death as a result of her drinking. She was emaciated and all of her organs were failing. My colleagues and I tried our best to help her stop drinking. We saw her in our offices, we saw her at her home, we even followed her into her favorite bar—all to no avail. Gail simply did not want to stop drinking. She died not long after. Don't let this be your life's story: if you have a substance abuse problem, get help before it's too late.

Sometimes the stereotype of the drunk or the drug addict keeps us from seeing that we have a problem. We think of an alcoholic as being a smelly street wino and so we say, "Oh, I'm not like that, so I can't be an alcoholic." We think of a drug addict as being a strung-out, homeless drifter and so we say, "Oh, that's not me, so I can't have a problem." These stereotypes can blind us from the truth. There are a great many alcoholics and addicts who have homes and jobs and function in their day-to-day lives. They get up in the morning, go to work or school, come home, go to bed—all of it under the influence of substances. Unlike the wino, the drifter or the runaway on the streets, they haven't lost everything—at least, not yet. If this is you, don't wait until it's too late to seek help.

Before we move on, let me summarize some important points. If you feel you have a substance abuse problem, seek help. If you are using substances and you feel yourself getting angry, leave the situation immediately—go somewhere by yourself and take a Time Out. If a friend or a family member is under the influence of a substance, don't choose that moment to talk to him/her about his/her abusive behavior. You'll just be wasting your breath. Wait until he/she is sober before discussing serious issues.

Teen Anger Assignment

At the end of this chapter you will find an Alcohol/Drug Log. Use this Log to record any experiences you may have with drugs and alcohol. Make photocopies of this Log for future use before you start. If you think back to chapter 9 of this book, you may remember that we talked about the **A-B-C**s of angry behavior. I said that every angry feeling had an **A**ntecedent (the thing that provoked it), manifested itself in **B**ehavior and had **C**onsequences. Our Alcohol/Drug Log will help you identify the **A-B-C**s of your substance use. First, write down in the log the antecedents of your substance use. What led you to drink or take drugs? Did you do it to fit in at a party? To relax? To numb feelings of pain? Then, write down your behavior. What did you do under the influence of alcohol/drugs? Did you get angry? Did you scream at people? Did you throw things? Last, write down the consequences of your behavior. What happened after your actions? Were you thrown out of the party? Were you grounded by your parents? Were you arrested?

The purpose of this exercise is to gather information about your substance use and help you see if it interferes with your attempts to manage your anger. The Log may also help you notice bad patterns in your behavior. For example, you may learn from it that you always feel the need to drink whenever you want to relax. Once you know this, you can brainstorm for other activities that might fill this need, such as exercising, meditation or sports activities. The Log will also help you notice if you are having trouble with peer pressure, a big problem for many adolescents. If this is true for you, remember the self-assertion skills we learned in the last chapter. Use these skills when you are in a peer-pressure situation. Take time now to imagine the next time your friends pressure you to take a drink or smoke a joint. Imagine yourself giving them a clear and simple "no." Remember that your true friends will respect your decision and accept you for who you are.

Be honest with yourself when you fill out the Log. Use the information to make discoveries about yourself and change your behavior for the better.

Alcohol/Drug Log

Date / Time:_____

Place: _____

What alcohol did you drink? How much? _____
_____

What drug(s) did you take? How much?_____
_____

What led up to your decision to drink/take drugs? _____
_____
_____

How did you behave after you drank/took drugs? _____
_____
_____

What were the consequences of your behavior?_____
_____
_____

How do you feel about the whole experience? _____
_____
_____

What could you have done differently?_____
_____
_____

Did you have problems managing your anger while under the influence
of drugs or alcohol? What were those problems? _____
_____
_____

Have you acted this way before? Do you see any patterns in your
behavior?_____
_____
_____

One more point: Think back to chapter 9 when we discussed "anger internalizers." These are people who cannot express their anger; they turn that anger on themselves rather than letting it out. Many of these "internalizers" use food rather than drugs or alcohol to cope with their pain. Quite naturally, this behavior can lead to a great many problems. If you are among those who use food to "medicate" yourself, the Alcohol/Drug Log can help you change your behavior. Simply cross out the references to alcohol and drugs and replace them with references to food and eating.

Teen Anger Tips

- The use of alcohol or drugs can greatly aggravate your anger problems.
- Alcohol and drugs weaken your self-control and make you more likely to act out on angry impulses.
- Withdrawal from substance use may also provoke angry responses.
- Some people *use* substances and some *abuse* them. There's a difference. If you abuse substances, you have a problem.
- If your family has a history of substance abuse problems, you are at an increased risk for having problems as well.
- If you aren't sure whether you have a problem, try to stop using substances for ninety days. If you can do it, you don't have a problem. If you can't, then you do.
- Substance abuse is not a problem you can stop on your own.
- Seek professional evaluation and assistance.
- There are a wide range of treatments available.
- Substance use can lead you to relapse into old forms of angry behavior.
- Use the Alcohol/Drug Log to find patterns in your substance use. Use this knowledge to change your behavior.
- Use the Log to discover why you feel the need to drink or take drugs. Learn to fill those needs with healthier activities.

part IV

Teen Anger Prescriptions

chapter 15

Shrinking Won't Make Your Head Smaller

You knew from the start that this wasn't for you
But your feelings can't control the things that you do.
- Mest, "Another Day"

As I said at the beginning of the book, when many teens first come to see me, I can tell that my office is the last place they want to be. Many of them have negative impressions about psychiatry and "shrinks." Some feel that coming to see me means they are in trouble or being held solely responsible for all of their families' problems. Their parents may not understand therapy themselves, expecting that I will automatically take their sides and tell their kids how to behave: "Go ahead, doctor, you tell them." The kids come in expecting to be lectured by some old guy with a beard and pipe so they look, feel and act very unhappy.

This is not how it is at all. I may be older, but I'm not that old. I don't have a beard (anymore) and I don't smoke a pipe (anymore). I have had success with teenagers, because I can understand and relate to them. If you decide to enter therapy, you may be pleasantly surprised to find that you and your counselor will be able to talk about the things important to you—things you may not have been able to express to others. Don't be intimidated! The purpose of therapy is not to give you another oppressive authority figure with whom you have to deal. The purpose is to give you someone to whom you can vent, a person who can understand your problems and help you handle and conquer them. Your therapist will understand that you are not to blame for all your family's problems—everyone in your family must share responsibility. The therapist is your ally, not your enemy.

The experience of one of my adolescent clients, Fred, may help you to gain realistic expectations of your therapy. Fred was a hyperactive teenager who was always getting in trouble at home. His parents brought him to therapy with the expectation that they could simply drop him off and let me "fix" him. Fred himself feared that I would take his parents' side and blame him for everything that had gone wrong. This was not the case at all. The first thing I noticed was that Fred only got in trouble at home and never at school. This led me to suspect that there was something wrong in the family dynamic that was provoking Fred's anger. I asked that Fred's entire family join us in our sessions. Soon I began to see that Fred's older brother Barry was part of the problem. Barry was the "good" son and he played this role with far too much enthusiasm. Barry would lecture Fred constantly, joining his parents in criticizing Fred and telling him how he should be. When this happened in our sessions, Fred would become restless and fidgety at first. Then he would start goofing around to try and change the subject. Then he would taunt Barry and call him a "nerd" and an "idiot." This only caused Barry to lecture him further. In total exasperation, Fred would finally get up and leave the room, slamming the door behind him.

We were able to deal with this problem pretty quickly. Each time Barry started to pick on his brother, I stopped him. Then I explained how Barry was provoking Fred to anger. I assigned their parents the responsibility of stopping Barry from acting like another parent. It was hard at first for Barry to stay out of the parenting business, but eventually he backed off. In time, the relationship between the two brothers improved and Fred's anger diminished.

The root of Fred's problem was the role he had assumed within the family. His brother Barry sought love and approval from their parents by being the "good" son. Fred knew he could never compete with Barry on this turf, so he decided to carve out his own territory as the "bad" son. By playing this role, Fred could at least attract negative attention to himself. I saw that this had to be corrected. I told Fred's parents to ignore Fred whenever he acted out. I told them to deny Fred the negative attention he was used to getting whenever he acted "bad." However, I also told them to praise their son and give him affection whenever he exhibited positive behavior. This broke the association in Fred's mind between acting out and parental attention. When Fred began to see he could only attract his parents' attention by acting positively, he stopped his destructive behavior. He no longer felt that he had to be the "bad" son.

Fred's story demonstrates two important things: First, don't assume that your therapist won't understand you. That's a therapist's job—to empathize with your problems and help you solve them. Second, don't assume that your therapist will take your parents' side and gang up with them against you. Therapists understand that sometimes it's the whole family that needs to work on changing. Fred solved his anger problems by working with a counselor to change how his family functioned and so can you.

Before we continue, I want to point out that this process isn't one where you can simply sit back and wait for everyone else to change. No, therapy requires you to work on yourself primarily. You'll probably find it similar to the experience of reading this book. Your therapist will give you assignments and teach you skills that you need to practice. Like Fred, you may have your family come into your sessions, although this is not always the case. Some families are unwilling to participate, in which case a therapist will work with you alone and help you to better cope with them. Sad to say, but it is usually those families who are unwilling to accept help that need it the most.

If you are the only member of your family trying to change, then reading this book may not be enough. You may need to seek outside professional help. If you can't talk to your parents about getting help, go to your school guidance counselor. Your counselor will be very familiar with the professionals in your community who are experienced in working with adolescents. He or she may also be able to help you talk to your parents about getting professional help. Your school system may even have its own mental health clinic. In the school district where I live, there are three schools that run clinics and offer up to six sessions of counseling. If more intensive help is needed, these clinics will refer students to outside professionals. Of course, this is only done with the student's consent.

Don't be afraid that the whole world will find out your secrets. Your confidentiality will be protected in therapy. A professional cannot discuss his or her client with a third party without that client's permission. This rule can only be broken if the client poses a danger to him/herself or others. In these extreme cases, the therapist must believe that the patient has specific violent plans and intent, as well as the means available, to do harm. So, for example, if the client says in a general way that he/she is thinking of suicide, the therapist will not lock up the client in a hospital. Everyone has these kinds of depressive feelings at times. In fact, these feelings are precisely the kinds of things that *should* be discussed with a therapist. If you decide to enter therapy, your counselor will explain all this in your first meeting.

This confidentiality between therapist and client is necessary to establish trust between them. Let's discuss your privacy issues with regard to your parents. Technically, parents are entitled to information about their child's treatment. However, professionals who work with teens know that the therapy will not be successful unless they set limits and boundaries to a parent's access to this information. In my case, I make it a point to never meet with parents unless the teen is also present. I don't want my teen clients to feel as though I'm talking about them behind their backs. Also, I inform everyone up-front about the importance of privacy and the limits of confidentiality. I explain to parents that the therapy will not work unless the discussions I have with their children are kept private. If a teen needs to share something with his/her parents, we do this as part of the treatment. In fact, I encourage my teens to do this themselves—I would rather my patients express their feelings directly to the people involved, rather than expressing their feelings to me and having me report those feelings to a third party.

Every so often I may have to give the parents a progress report, but I will always keep this general. I'll say something like "Yes, your child is making progress," or "No, we're not clicking. Maybe we should consider a referral to another therapist." If I feel that the teen poses a real, specific threat and imminent danger to him/herself or others, I will discuss this with the parents, but only with the teen present. I do this because this matter is too important not to discuss openly. In the cases where this happens, the teen usually resents the intervention at the time, but later becomes extremely thankful that I brought his/her pain out into the open and dealt with it. Except for these rare cases, I make sure to preserve the confidentiality between myself and my teen clients. If you go to see a therapist, you can be sure that he or she will do the same for you.

In this chapter we've gone over what therapy is and what it can do for you if you are having serious anger problems. Remember that the therapist is your ally, someone you can trust to understand your problems and help you through them. If you feel that you would like to talk to a counselor, ask your parents about it. If you feel you can't discuss your desire to see a therapist with your parents, go to your school's guidance counselor. You don't have to solve your problems alone. If you want help, all you need to do is ask for it. Sometimes that seems difficult, but often it is the first step toward making positive changes in your life.

Teen Anger Tips

- ◆ If your anger problems are too much for you to deal with on your own, a therapist can help you.
- ◆ Therapy will specifically address your personal needs and circumstances.
- ◆ Therapy is successful only when you commit yourself to work for change.
- ◆ Therapy is not for "crazy" people.
- ◆ Your treatment will be private and confidential.

chapter 16

Catastrophic Stress/Catastrophic Anger

And still I see no changes; Can't a brother get a little peace?
It's war on the streets and war in the Middle East
- Tupac Shakur, "Changes"

I first learned of the horrific terrorist attacks of September 11, 2001 from my father. He called me and said, "Something terrible has happened. Two airliners crashed into the World Trade Center towers and the Pentagon was also attacked." I immediately flashed back to the day President Kennedy was assassinated. At the time, I was in the third grade at P.S. 105 in the Bronx, New York. The voice of our principal, Mr. Stark, came over the loud speaker in the classroom. He told us what had happened and that school was being closed. As I began to walk the four blocks home from school, I noticed something strange: the streets were filled with people in the middle of the day. It seemed like absolutely no one was at work or in school. Usually the streets were deserted, but now they were bustling with people walking around stunned or frightened. It just did not seem real. Then I saw my Dad walking toward me on the sidewalk. I was surprised and glad to see him. Suddenly I felt safer and more secure.

I will always remember that day, just as many of you will always remember what you were doing on September 11. When we live through a catastrophe, we often alternate between periods of disbelief, sadness and anger. This kind of an event takes a long time to get over. The loss we all felt on September 11, 2001 will not heal quickly.

What is the correct way to respond to a catastrophe like that which occurred on that tragic day in September? There is no right answer.

Sometimes it's easier to deal with the issue in an intellectual way—to talk about world terrorism and what response the country should take. Sometimes it seems right to deal with the issue emotionally. Sometimes we shift back and forth between these two responses. All of this is perfectly normal. Sometimes it helps to give voice to our angry thoughts and vent how we feel. This too can be helpful; as long as we remember that we must only express these feelings in words and never in actions. When it was revealed that the September 11 attacks had been committed by Islamic terrorists, some Americans vented their anger by attacking peaceful Muslim citizens of our own country. Actions such as these diminish us all.

The anger we feel in response to catastrophic events is acceptable, understandable and normal. As I've said several times before, the important thing is how we choose to express our anger. All of the anger management techniques we've learned thus far can help us control our anger during times of both extreme national crises as well as personal ones.

Take note of how our nation responded in the wake of the attacks. We did not leap or rush into action. Our government leaders set aside anger and approached the problem in thoughtful, patient ways. In fact, President Bush used many of the techniques we've discussed in this book:

1. **Assertion.** The President asserted our position by demanding that the Taliban turn over Osama bin Laden or lose power.
2. **Communication.** The President communicated his intentions to the country by giving a televised speech before a joint session of Congress.
3. **Negotiation.** The President negotiated with other nations to form a coalition against terrorism.

Let our nation's measured response to that day be a model for how you can manage your anger after a catastrophic event.

In the first week after the attack, my patients spoke of nothing else. We all needed to vent. Talking is therapeutic, because it allows us to feel heard and understood. When catastrophe strikes, it is important to talk with your loved ones. Listen to your family and friends. Express your feelings. You can do this in words or through artistic expression. Write a poem, compose a song or do a drawing. This last mode of expression can be especially helpful for young children. One six-year-old I know spontaneously drew a picture of an airplane and a tall building with people falling out of it. This expression of her feelings was frightening but therapeutic. It's important that you express through words or images the feelings you have after a catastrophic event. Don't be afraid to cry in front of others. Let your friends know that it's okay for them to cry. Don't deny your feelings—express them.

Immediately after hearing about the attacks I felt the need to help others. As a member of the Army Reserve, I made a telephone call and offered my assistance. This made me feel useful and involved. By helping others, I realized I could help myself as well. When catastrophe strikes, channel your anger into this kind of action. Brainstorm by yourself and with your family about what each of you can do to help. Many people did exactly that in the wake of the September 11 attacks. Thousands of public safety personnel flocked to New York to help with the rescue efforts. Tens of thousands of ordinary people gave blood, prayed, donated money and participated in rallies or religious services. Taking action helped us to cope with our grief.

Catastrophes come in all shapes and sizes. Often, everyday people face enormous adversities in their lives that result in catastrophic stress and anger. R.J., one of my clients, experienced more trauma in his youth than most people do in a lifetime.

R.J. was thirteen when he came to see me. His little brother, Joey, had been born with a rare genetic disorder and was not expected to live beyond the age of three. Joey was totally disabled; he did not speak, walk, feed himself or talk. The small apartment R.J. shared with his mother and Joey was so crowded with special equipment and machines for Joey that it looked like a hospital.

Ever since he was born, the boys' mother's life centered around Joey. R.J. had been forced to take a backseat to his brother's needs. He could not make too many demands or cause any stress for his mother. The boys' father was not available to R.J. either. The man had a nervous breakdown as a result of Joey's condition. He could not cope and left R.J. and his mom alone to deal with Joey's illness. R.J. did his best to be strong for his mother as "the man of the house." He was forced to become mature beyond his years.

In time, Joey's organs began failing one by one. Despite the best efforts of doctors and Joey's mom, the young boy died at home with his mother and brother by his side. R.J.'s mom had a very healthy attitude about the loss. She knew she was powerless and accepted it. Even though her outlook was good for R.J., the loss of his little brother was still a profoundly difficult experience for him.

R.J.'s grades began to slip. No longer having to be the perfect child, R.J. was unsure of his identity and began questioning things. *Why keep living as before? What is life supposed to be like?* Now he felt he had choices and freedom. They now had more resources, both financial and emotional. *How would they live?* R.J. and his mom were both struggling to find new identities. Whereas their identities had been defined by Joey's illness in the past, now things were different.

R.J. went through a phase of trying new options. It was rocky. His mom needed help adjusting and coping with R.J. We worked together to keep the lines of communication open between the two of them. R.J.'s mom tried to give him more attention than she could when Joey was alive, but this meant less freedom for R.J., something he was not used to or happy about. R.J. was used to fending for himself and now he had a full-time parent watching over him. His mom learned that she couldn't suddenly change the rules on him and tried not to focus too intensely on R.J.'s every action. She reminded herself that R.J. was not Joey and didn't need her constant supervision.

In time, R.J. and his mom settled into new roles. R.J. began to appreciate their time together and the freedom his mom was still allowing him to have. Happier at home, he was able to focus more on his schoolwork. Free of the burdens of helping to care for his brother and be the "man of the house," R.J. made the transition back to being an average teenager.

The story of R.J. and his mom shows that catastrophes often change our lives in such a way that who we were before is different from the person we become after the tragic event. Most people today, when discussing topics from politics to entertainment, think or talk in terms of "before 9/11" and "after 9/11." That date has become a marker of a time when everybody's lives changed. After catastrophes, we go through a period of tremendous transitions and adjustments. Even with the passage of time, hurt and pain can linger, especially if we have difficulty dealing with the transitions that result. It is important to utilize coping techniques like expressing your feelings, performing constructive acts, listening to others and helping those in need. And when these coping techniques are not enough to get you through the trauma and the difficult period that follows it, you may need to seek professional counseling.

Catastrophic Stress/Catastrophic Anger Journal

If you ever have the misfortune of living through a catastrophe, write down what you are feeling. When you are done, put your writing and your feelings aside for the moment. Distract yourself from your feelings for a period of time. Balance your response between periods of thought, feeling and constructive action.

_____

_____

_____

_____

_____
_____
_____
_____
_____
_____
_____
_____
_____
_____
_____
_____
_____
_____
_____
_____
_____
_____

Constructive Acts

In the wake of a catastrophe, brainstorm for some positive, healthy actions you might take to help you cope with your feelings. At the end of the exercise, write down a commitment to perform at least one positive action each week.

1) _____
_____
_____

2) _____
_____
_____

3) _____
_____
_____

Commitment: _____

_____

_____

_____

Terror-Based Irrational Thoughts

Think back to chapter 10, when we discussed the subject of irrational thoughts. Catastrophic events can often cause us to think irrationally. This exercise teaches skills to counter irrational thoughts by using the example of the September 11 terrorist attacks against our country. First, read the examples. Then, write down an irrational thought you had. Last, dispute it.

Thought:
"Never trust anyone of Islamic faith."
Disputation:
"I'm overgeneralizing. There were many members of the Islamic faith who were as hurt by the terrorist attacks of September 11 as I was."

Thought:
"There is a Mosque in our town. I should get my friends and we'll go bust some windows."
Disputation:
"I feel anger, but I am not going to act out violently against others. Then the terrorists will have won."

Thought:

_____

_____

Disputation:

_____

_____

Thought:

_____

_____

Disputation:

_____

_____

Thought:

_____

_____

Disputation:

_____

_____

Thought:

_____

_____

Disputation:

_____

_____

Teen Anger Tips

- When catastrophe strikes, whether on a national scale or a personal one, our feelings can fluctuate from disbelief to sadness to anger. All this is perfectly normal.
- Expressing a desire for revenge can be a way to vent feelings of outrage.
- It's okay to express anger in words—it's not okay to act on it.
- Use our government's method of handling the 9/11 disaster as a positive model for how to cope with catastrophe.
- Use art as a way to express your feelings. Paint a picture, compose a song or write in your journal.
- Encourage and help children to express their feelings after the event.
- Check in with yourself and others periodically.
- Try to help other victims after the catastrophic event— doing something positive will help you control your anger.
- Even after the event has passed, there will be a difficult transition period; it is helpful to keep looking for opportunities to contribute, to come together and to share your emotions with others.

chapter 17

Why Did My Parents Have to Ruin My Life? Sibling Rivalry and Anger

Now I got no patience,
So sick of complacence,
With the D the E the F the I the A the N the C the E...
- Rage Against the Machine, "Know Your Enemy"

One of the most common anger problems that families come to see me about is sibling rivalry. Fighting between siblings is commonplace in both functional and dysfunctional families. Although this kind of rivalry is perfectly normal, it can be a source of great stress to parents and kids alike.

Sibling rivalry may be common, but *how* and *why* siblings fight will vary greatly from family to family. This may be due to such factors as the number of siblings, their genders, their age differences and whether they are biological or stepsiblings. However, these situations all share in common the same intense and seemingly endless fighting. Whether verbal or physical, this fighting is usually provoked by a single emotion: anger. Siblings can become angry over a whole host of issues, such as:

1. Competition for their parents' attention.
2. Conflict over the borrowing of each other's stuff.
3. Dissatisfaction cause by a younger sibling hanging around an older sibling and his/her friends.
4. Resentment when an older sibling is forced to baby-sit or watch out for a younger sibling.
5. Tension when one sibling assumes the role of a parent over another (as in the case of Barry and Fred).

6. Indignation when one sibling assumes the role of the "good child" and another the "bad child" (again, as in the case of Barry and Fred).
7. Jealousy between siblings.
8. Low self-esteem causing one sibling to act out negatively toward another.
9. Displaced anger due to anger each sibling feels going unexpressed.

When siblings fight, it's in everyone's interest to resolve the problem. Wouldn't you be happier if you could do away with bad feelings toward a brother or sister once and for all? Since it's not likely that your parents are going to send away your sibling for good, you're going to have to deal with this problem whether you like it or not.

Dennis, one of my clients, had serious problems with his siblings. At seventeen, he was a high school senior, captain of the football team and an honor student. He also had been verbally and physically abusing his girlfriend for two years. His girlfriend finally told her parents and Dennis' parents about the abuse.

When Dennis came to see me, he was desperate for help. We first worked to get his anger under control, then we focused on the reasons behind his abuse of his girlfriend. I learned he did not grow up in a violent home, nor did he witness abuse. His parents didn't even argue much. Finally, Dennis came to realize his abusive behavior had to do with his birth order.

Dennis was the eldest of three boys. He grew up physically dominating his younger brothers. When he wanted something and they refused, Dennis used his size and strength to put them in their place and get what he wanted. It always worked. Just like that, his behavior was reinforced by his success and Dennis' aggression developed. Dennis carried this aggression on to the football field, into friendships and into his relationship with his girlfriend. He dominated and controlled her with his sheer brute force.

Dennis came to me feeling terrible about himself, but he learned he was not a bad person. He had learned and retained bad behaviors. We worked together to help him unlearn them and develop a new repertoire of effective communication and negotiation skills. As a result, he rebuilt his relationship with his girlfriend. He also learned to interact positively with his brothers who then became more than just siblings; they became his friends.

As has been mentioned before, you only have control over the things *you* do. You cannot control another person. Don't sit around waiting for your sibling to change the situation—focus on yourself and make the changes *you* need to make. Try to think of three things you can do to improve your relationship with your sibling. Stay focused on what *you* can do to alleviate the problem. What your sibling must do is up to him/her, so concentrate instead on the things that are within your power to change.

If you are lucky, your sibling will be willing to work things out with you. Try to set up a meeting and negotiate your way out of the conflict. Use all of the techniques we learned back in chapter 14. Brainstorm together for constructive solutions and try to reach an agreement. Try paraphrasing each other's statements. If you begin arguing again, call a Time Out. You may eventually need to call someone else in to mediate your dispute. This person should act like an impartial referee and decline to take one side over another.

When negotiating with your sibling, be sure to express how you feel, but also remember to listen to how your sibling feels. If you truly listen to someone else, that person will be much more likely to do the same for you. Also, remember the spirit of compromise: you must give up something to get something. Each party must change his/her behavior in order to achieve a lasting peace.

If you and your sibling can manage to agree to a contract, put it in writing. Then make sure you honor your side of the bargain. Don't think that the contract alone will solve all of your problems—both of you still have to make the effort to follow the contract and get along. This won't be easy, but you can do it—so long as you both consciously change your attitude toward the other and agree to work together. Often this shift of attitude is the most important step in solving the problem. Making a conscious effort to act better toward the other person will improve your relations and reduce your own stress.

Teen Anger Exercise

In the space provided, list any problems you are currently having with your sibling(s). What do you argue over? What do you fight about? Write it all down.

1. _____

_____

_____

2. _____

_____

_____

3. _____

_____

_____

Now brainstorm for ideas on what you can do to resolve each of these problems:

1. a._____

_____

b._____

_____

c._____

_____

2. a._____

_____

b._____

_____

c._____

_____

3. a._____

_____

b._____

_____

c._____

_____

If your sibling wants to work with you, have him/her write down what he/she can do to resolve each problem:

1. a._____

_____

b. _____

_____

c. _____

_____

2. a. _____

_____

b. _____

_____

c. _____

_____

3. a. _____

_____

b. _____

_____

c. _____

_____

If any of these problems involve your parents, you may want to ask them to join your negotiations. Ask them what they might do to help resolve the problem. Once you've completed your list, act on the suggestions. Have each person display his/her list in a prominent place so that it stays fresh in everyone's memory.

Teen Sibling Contract

Write a contract for you and your sibling(s). Compile all of the lists you've written and draw up a complete statement that outlines what each person agrees to do. If you like, you can involve your parents as well. Make sure each party signs the contract.

We agree to do the following: _____

_____

_____

_____

_____

_____

_____

_____

_____

_____

_____

_____

_____

_____

Signed:_____   Signed:_____

Signed:_____   Signed:_____

Teen Anger Prescription

To avoid future conflicts with siblings, you may want to hold a family conference on sibling rivalry and relations once a week to discuss problems and issues. Schedule it for the same day and time each week and make sure both you, your siblings and other family members if you wish, participate. Allow no interruptions. Meet every week, even if there seems to be no sibling problem to talk about—siblings can check in with each other and discuss positive things as well. When siblings are having problems, address them in these meetings. State the problem clearly and allow everyone to brainstorm for possible solutions. Sometimes it is enough to just allow a sibling to talk about the problem and release pent-up emotions. The structure of a sibling conference can allow you to assert yourself and express your anger constructively. If you and your siblings work together in these conferences, you will find that your rivalry will diminish.

All of these techniques are excellent ways to reduce sibling rivalry. However, sometimes these techniques are not enough and professional help is needed. This was the case with Fred and Barry—their rivalry was a symptom of a deeper family problem. This was also true of another case that I'd like to tell you about. I had to use all of my detective skills to get to the bottom of this one.

Seth, my client, was thirteen years old and the middle child of three. His older brother was fifteen and his younger sister was seven. Their parents were both highly educated. In fact, the father was a psychologist like I am. You see, even therapists have problems we need help solving. Everyone in the family was a high achiever. The parents had been excellent students and had grown up never getting into trouble. The brother and sister were also excellent students and similarly never had serious problems. Yet Seth was just an average student who constantly got in trouble for talking in classes and goofing around at home. He sought attention by being a clown. He did this because he didn't feel he could compete with his siblings in their academic studies. So Seth looked for self-esteem in more interactive ways. This did not go over well with the rest of the family, who tended to be less extroverted and didn't value practical jokes.

Seth felt he didn't fit in with the other members of his family. In fact, he was right about this. His family did not accept him, because he was so different. This lack of acceptance created a vicious cycle: the more Seth acted up, the angrier his family got. The angrier he got his family, the less they accepted him. The less they accepted him, the more he acted up.

Suddenly the case turned into a detective novel. Someone in the family started trashing Seth's room on a regular basis. This mystery person repeatedly destroyed his things and stole some of his expensive prize possessions. Things got so bad that Seth's parents finally put a lock on his door. A few days after this, Seth's little sister became the prime suspect in the case—some of Seth's possessions were found hidden in her room. The problem was that no one could understand how she managed to get past the lock or when she had the time to perpetrate her crimes. Seth's sister was with the family all day, yet Seth returned to his room and still found his things destroyed.

Seth's parents became very concerned about their daughter. They started taking her for therapy to find out why their good little girl had suddenly become a master thief and vandal. They repeatedly grounded her in an attempt to solve the problem, but the trashings continued. No sooner did Seth's sister end her punishment then a mysterious attack on Seth's room occurred yet again.

I had a theory about what was really going on, but I remained silent. Sometimes a therapist needs to act dumb, not smart. I thought it would be best if I let the truth of the situation emerge on its own. In fact, that is exactly what happened. After awhile, Seth became so guilt-ridden that he could not contain himself anymore and came clean. During one session while his father was present, Seth confessed that he'd been destroying his own stuff and framing his sister by planting his things in her room. Seth tearfully explained that he did this to shift attention away from himself. He hated constantly being under the spotlight of family scrutiny, criticism and punishment. He wanted out. Of course, he had to sacrifice his sister to accomplish this and his guilt over this fact finally caused him to confess.

Seth created a false sibling rivalry to improve his position in the family pecking order. His parents did not severely punish him after he told the truth, because they finally realized how badly he needed to be accepted. They made the effort to see the value of Seth's talents. Although these gifts were very different from theirs, they were equally as valuable. Soon Seth enrolled in acting classes and became quite a good performer. Seth desperately needed to excel and be appreciated for who he was. When Seth's parents finally learned to accept him, his relationship with his siblings improved dramatically.

Thus we see that sibling rivalry can often be the symptom of larger family problems. If you feel you can't control your relationship with your sibling(s), your family may need to enter therapy together. However, the techniques we've discussed in this chapter will be very helpful in solving your sibling problems. One we talked about earlier is important. Try to work things out by stating the problem clearly and brainstorming for solutions. Your life will become a whole lot easier if you make the effort to resolve the sibling rivalry problem in this way.

Teen Anger Tips

- Sibling rivalry occurs in most families.
- The root of the problem is anger. Solve this problem by using anger management techniques.
- Don't obsess over how your sibling is causing the problem. Focus on what you can do to solve the problem.
- Write down ways you can make things better.
- If your sibling is willing, work together to draw up a contract. Write down what each party will do to resolve the conflict.
- Hold regular sibling conferences to address issues and brainstorm for solutions.
- When you fight with your siblings, use the anger management skills that we've learned so far: relaxation, Time Outs, assertion and clear communication.

chapter 18

Jerks: Blended Families and Anger

I don't want to have to split the holidays
I don't want two addresses
I don't want a stepbrother anyways
And I don't want my mom to have to change her last name...
- Pink, "Family Portrait"

So, is your new stepfather a jerk? Are you and your new stepmother constantly fighting? Does it seem like your stepbrothers and stepsisters are from another planet? I understand. Hearing about stepfamilies (or "blended families," as they are sometimes called) always makes me think of the scene in the movie *St. Elmo's Fire*, in which Demi Moore's character refers to her father's new wife as being her step-*monster*.

Nevertheless, blended families are very common today though they can be the scene for some very emotionally charged interactions. After all, when you become part of a stepfamily, your life has been turned upside-down by divorce or a parent's death and now you have to deal with a whole new family you do not know and may not like when you meet them. You may have new stepbrothers and stepsisters living in your home or even in your room. Your new stepdad, who seemed so nice when he was just dating your mom, may now act like a raving lunatic. Your new stepmom may seem like she's always annoyed to see you. With all this going on, do people actually expect you to be able to concentrate on your schoolwork?

One organization that tries to help in situations like these is the Stepfamily Association of America. This group serves as a resource for blended families and sponsors a national network of support groups. It also produces a monthly newsletter and other educational materials. If your blended family is having trouble, ask one of your parents to contact this association through their web site, www.saafamilies.org or by calling 1-800-735-0329 for more information.

Sometimes the problems in blended families are so complicated and intense that professional help is needed. In such a case, you may need to enter a support group or seek family counseling. If you feel your family ought to go in this direction, a good time to raise the subject is during a family conference.

Whenever blended families come to see me, I always try to discuss discipline and relationship issues with the parents. Children need discipline, yet effective discipline can only come out of a loving relationship. If that loving relationship is not there, discipline will only serve to antagonize and drive the child away. Since it may take a long time for a stepparent and a stepchild to form a caring relationship, I always advise that the biological parent be the disciplinarian. The stepparent should only offer advice on disciplinary matters. I also tell the stepparent that it is his/her responsibility to establish a relationship with the stepchild and not the other way around. I tell the kids that it's not their jobs to set up relationships with their stepparents. Let your stepparent come to you—but when he or she does, be sure to reciprocate.

Kyle and Kelly, two teens with whom I worked, began having problems at home a few months after their mom, Wendy, married John. Kyle and Kelly had been through a lot. Their parents were divorced and did not get along. Often when their father came to pick them up or drop them off for visitation, he would get into an argument with Wendy or John. Furthermore, their mother and stepfather openly and heatedly argued at length about Kyle and Kelly's father's failure to pay child support. In addition to all of this conflict, their biological father often did not exercise his visitation rights. He simply wouldn't show up or call for weeks on end leaving Kyle and Kelly to wonder what happened to him.

To add fuel to the fire, John was a strict disciplinarian who had unrealistic expectations of his teenaged stepchildren. When arguments ensued, Wendy often defended her children which only caused John to yell at her. Despite the fact that their mother usually sided with them, Kyle and Kelly became more and more angry with her. The reason? She was the only one at whom they could safely direct their anger. They were afraid of John, who had bad temper and could be intimidating. Their father also had a bad temper and besides, Kyle and Kelly reasoned, if they expressed anger towards him, he might abandon all contact with them completely.

It was clear to me that the adults in Kyle and Kelly's lives were not good role models for expressing angry feelings in healthy ways. Their father and John lashed out at others in anger and their mother remained passive, bottling it all up inside. When Kyle and Kelly weren't dumping their anger on their mom, they were fighting with each other. The entire family needed help...fast!

As sometimes happens, John and Wendy dumped Kyle and Kelly in therapy to be "fixed" by me. I convinced John and Wendy that although Kyle and Kelly needed to improve their abilities to deal with negative feelings, the entire family needed fixing. Reluctantly, they agreed to participate in therapy.

Through individual counseling, I helped Kyle and Kelly acknowledge their feelings so they could see how their emotions effected their actions. They realized that their actions and rivalry were a result of bottling up resentment, anger, frustration and hurt feelings. They had made attacking their mom and each other their only safe outlets for expressing their anger. Instead, through counseling they learned to talk about their feelings and develop methods to effectively express them without hurting others.

In family therapy, I helped John and Wendy become more receptive to listening to each other's and the children's feelings when those feelings were being expressed constructively. In addition, Wendy was put in charge of disciplining the children while John was assigned the job of simply focusing on developing a more positive relationship with his stepchildren. Most importantly, the family agreed to hold weekly conferences to discuss issues, problems and good things as well. They all promised to work on reaching compromises.

As a result, John and Wendy got better not only at handling problems with the children, but with each other and with Wendy's ex-husband. They became better role models in dealing with their feelings in constructive ways. Kyle and Kelly could now look to their mother and stepfather for advice, support and guidance. This reduced stress and brought peace to their household.

If your blended family is having problems like the ones experienced by Kyle and Kelly, call for a family conference right now and read this chapter out loud together. Use the information here to open up discussion and make some positive changes. The anger management skills we've learned so far will improve communication and reduce conflict. Most importantly, complete the next exercise. Working together as a group on this exercise will go a long way toward helping your family solve its problems.

Solving Problems in Blended Families

Have each member of your family make a list of the problems that he/she thinks your blended family is having. Ask everyone to be as specific as possible and use real examples from your daily family life. You may use the space that follows; have your family members use blank sheets of paper:

1. _____
   _____

2. _____
   _____

3. _____
   _____

4. _____
   _____

5. _____
   _____

After everyone has finished, read the list you've compiled to the group. Then allow the other kids in the family to read their lists. Finally, give your parents their turn.

Now that each person has voiced his/her concerns, have the family brainstorm together for possible solutions to each problem. Start with your list first. Re-read problem #1 out loud and ask everyone for ideas on how to solve it. Write those ideas in the space provided. After you are finished, move on to problem #2 and work down your list:

1.   a. _____
     b. _____
     c. _____
     d. _____

2.   a. _____
     b. _____
     c. _____
     d. _____

3.   a. _____
     b. _____
     c. _____
     d. _____

4. a. _____
   b. _____
   c. _____
   d. _____

5. a. _____
   b. _____
   c. _____
   d. _____

Don't work on your list only—remember to work on your family members' lists as well. Use separate sheets of paper to brainstorm for solutions to those problems.

After you have finished brainstorming, try to agree as a group on the *best* solution for each problem. Re-read the possible solutions and debate the pros and cons of each proposal. Come to some agreement on which solution is best. Be fair and honest when making this decision. Go back to your list and *circle* the solution that everyone agrees on.

If your family has come this far in the exercise, you have achieved a great deal. Everyone should now agree on what your family's problems are and how you should go about solving them. In the space which follows, each family member will write down what he or she needs to do to make these solutions work. What changes need to be made? What promises need to be kept? Write the answer to all these questions down and display the list you've worked on together in a prominent place to keep it fresh in everyone's memory:

You
1. _____
2. _____
3. _____
4. _____

Your biological parent
1. _____
2. _____
3. _____
4. _____

Your stepparent

1. _____
2. _____
3. _____
4. _____

Your sibling/stepsibling: _____
(**write sibling's name here**)

1. _____
2. _____
3. _____
4. _____

Your sibling/stepsibling: _____
(**write sibling's name here**)

1. _____
2. _____
3. _____
4. _____

Your sibling/stepsibling: _____
(**write sibling's name here**)

1. _____
2. _____
3. _____
4. _____

Your sibling/stepsibling: _____
(**write sibling's name here**)

1. _____
2. _____
3. _____
4. _____

Now that each family member knows what is required of him/her, draw up a contract that outlines this new agreement. Write down in specific detail what each party promises to do in order to end the conflict and improve relations. Remember to compromise: give something in order to get something. Have everyone involved sign the contract.

Contract

_____
_____
_____
_____
_____
_____
_____
_____
_____
_____
_____
_____
_____
_____

Signed:_____   Signed:_____

Signed:_____   Signed:_____

Signed:_____   Signed:_____

I hope this exercise has helped your family clarify its problems and get on the right track to solving them. Here are some additional exercises to help you all work together more effectively.

Teen Anger Exercise: Time Out Dry-run

As we've discussed before, the Time Out is an excellent anger management tool. Sit down with your blended family and explain how a Time Out works. Then role-play a practice Time Out. It's a good idea to practice this while everyone is calm so that all will know what to do when things get heated. In your role-play, have someone pretend to start an argument. Then allow someone to call a Time Out and leave the room. The person who calls the Time Out should go off and do something relaxing. The people left behind should engage in something relaxing as well. After awhile, the person who called the Time Out should reconvene with the family to discuss how the Time Out went. If there were any problems, brainstorm for solutions. Practice again. You might consider making these dry-runs a weekly exercise. Practicing a Time Out every week will make it more likely that it will work at the moment you really need it to.

The Floor Exercise

Have a family conference. Take a pillow and give it to the person who speaks first. Explain that no one can talk unless that person holds the pillow. Everyone else must listen. When the speaker is done, he or she should place the pillow in the middle of the group. Then the next speaker picks it up and has the floor. Remember: you may not talk unless you hold the pillow. This rule will help if your family conferences tend to get rambunctious.

Respect

Everyone wants to be treated with respect. In order to get it, you must give it, so treat others with respect. Treat others how you would like to be treated. Make up your mind to rise above conflicts and act with a regard for higher values. If you've acted in a way that later makes you feel ashamed or guilty, that's a clear sign that you need to change your behavior. Act in ways that will later make you feel good about yourself.

All of these techniques can go a long way toward improving communication inside your blended family. However, there are some situations that require outside intervention and help. As an example of this, let me tell you about a former patient of mine named Mary Beth.

Mary Beth came to me for help when she was seventeen. She and her older sister had lived alone with their mom until Mary Beth was ten. Then her mom met a man named Alfred and married him just five weeks later. Alfred had been pleasant toward the children during those first five weeks. However, on the very day of the wedding, Alfred verbally abused his new stepchildren. Mary Beth remembers how her heart sank on that day. She and her sister knew they were going to have trouble. They just didn't know how bad it would be.

It turned out that Alfred was a functional alcoholic. He got up and went to work everyday, but drank almost constantly. Mary Beth's mom worked hard to cover Alfred's drinking problem. There were many mornings when Mary Beth and her mother went out looking for Alfred's car, because he couldn't remember where he had parked it during his drunken binge the previous night. When one person aids another in his/her drinking problem, that person is called an "enabler." Mary Beth's mom was an enabler and Mary Beth herself became an enabler at the age of sixteen. After she got her driver's license, she drove Alfred and his golf buddies to the country club so they could drink.

On top of the drinking, Alfred was emotionally and physically abusive. He constantly put Mary Beth down and criticized her. He disciplined her by hitting her with a thick leather belt with a heavy steel buckle. Worst of all, Alfred sexually abused Mary Beth. The first time he molested her was when she was just eleven.

When Mary Beth first came to see me, I guessed that her mother was also a recipient of Alfred's abusive behavior. However, Mary Beth was very unwilling to talk about how her mom was being treated at home. It seemed as though Mary Beth thought that the two of them were victims together and that she was somehow protecting her mother by keeping quiet. Mary Beth's mom enabled her husband's alcoholism and abuse and Mary Beth enabled her mother by keeping quiet about it all. Of course, all of this caused Mary Beth to become extremely angry, but she wouldn't allow herself to recognize her anger. She just stuffed it down and eventually turned it against herself.

Mary Beth's mother dealt with her husband's abuse by becoming passive and trying to ignore it. She devoted herself to maintaining the fiction that everything was alright. She swept all issues and problems under the rug. Anything not to upset Alfred. When Mary Beth went to her mother at age eleven about the molestation, her mom's only response was to say: "Stay away from him when he's drinking." Quite simply, Mary Beth's mom was unwilling to recognize the severity of the problem. This caused Mary Beth to feel very conflicted. On the one hand, Mary Beth loved her mother and identified with her as a fellow victim of Alfred's abuse. On the other hand, Mary Beth felt emotionally abandoned by her mother because she had refused to protect her. These feelings of abandonment were as damaging to Mary Beth as the abuse itself. The effects of all of this continued up through Mary Beth's adulthood and required a lot of therapy to undo. It is to Mary Beth's credit that she survived emotionally.

Because Mary Beth did not allow herself to recognize her anger, that anger festered inside her for years until she finally turned it against herself. Mary Beth embarked on a very self-destructive path in her late teen years. It was as though she had told herself, "My stepdad treats me like trash and my mom doesn't care, so why should I care either?" She stopped caring about school, partied heavily and got into destructive relationships with guys. She rebelled at school as a way of calling attention to herself. She put all of her energy into her social life, because her friends were her only source of emotional support. As she said at the time, "I know my friends care about me."

Mary Beth was very courageous to come and seek help on her own. In our work together, she was able to acknowledge both what had been done to her and her angry feelings about it. She learned to stop acting out her anger in destructive ways. Mary Beth cannot change her past, but she has learned how to cope with it.

If you are being abused, you can end your silence just as Mary Beth did. If you are reading this book and suffering from abuse, put the book down and go tell someone. Right now. Tell one your parents. If your parent does nothing about the situation, tell one of your teachers or friends. The person abusing you may have threatened violence against you if you talk. Nevertheless, you must tell someone. Alfred had told Mary Beth, "Of course, your mother should never know anything about this." Remember that you are not helping anyone by remaining silent. You must put a stop to the abuse and the first step is to tell someone about what is going on.

People who sexually molest and abuse children are committing illegal acts and must be prosecuted by law to stop them from hurting anyone ever again. The law can prosecute these criminals even years after the abuse occurred. Sounds drastic? Not as drastic as the damage that abuse causes in a child's life. The authorities will be willing to listen to you and take action to stop the abuse. Stand up for yourself. If you are being abused, take advantage of the law and protect yourself.

Teen Anger Tips

- The Stepfamily Association of America is an excellent resource for education about how to solve problems inside blended families.
- If your blended family is having trouble, you might consider joining a support group or entering family counseling.
- Only the biological parent should discipline the child. The stepparent should work on establishing a caring relationship with the stepchild.
- Use family conferences to discuss and resolve problems.
- Have your family list problems and brainstorm for solutions.
- Have each family member keep his or her own "To Do" list.
- Write contracts.
- Practice Time-Outs as a family.
- Use the Floor Exercise to help communication.
- Try giving respect to get respect.
- If you are being abused, stop being silent. Tell someone about what is happening to you.

chapter 19

School Shooters:
Bullying, Teasing, Rejection and Anger

I don't want you and I don't need you,
don't bother to resist, I'll beat you.
It's not your fault that you're always wrong,
the weak ones are there to justify the strong.
- Marilyn Manson, "The Beautiful People"

The tragic incident at Columbine High School, where two students decided that they would "get revenge" by shooting classmates they felt had rejected them, is an unforgettable one. The crimes which occurred there were an extreme example of acting out on the rage children can feel when they are bullied, teased and rejected.

Unfortunately, bullying is commonplace in too many schools, because sadly some teens use it as a method to form their identity as individuals. In my practice, I have helped many teens cope with being bullied and picked on. Most teens come to know themselves through their membership in a group or clique. All too often, teens can be very fanatical about defining who is in the popular group and who is not. After all, being accepted in a group feels wonderful. So people inside the group will often try to protect this wonderful feeling by reminding the outsiders of their excluded status. Doing this reinforces the insider's sense of being a group member: *I know that I am "in" because I have the power to tell you that you are "out."*

As I've said before, adolescence is a very insecure time. Teens are changing from children to adults and this transition is not easy. As they change, some teens feel they have to get to know themselves all over again. Different individuals will try on different personas to see what fits and what doesn't. Many teens seek to minimize their insecurities by finding acceptance in a group. This has always been the case. When I was in high school, my classmates divided themselves up into the brains, the jocks, the preps and the greasers. Your high school may have groups like basers, rockers, surfers and Goths. Whatever the group, the purpose behind them is the same: to help teens find themselves by identifying with their peers. Some teens completely lose their individual identity in a group. Some teens float between groups. Some never join a group at all—this can often be a lonely and difficult path to follow.

Acceptance is a very emotionally charged issue in adolescence. In fact, emotions can run so high during these years that teens often behave very cruelly toward one another. As I mentioned above, people who are accepted in a group seek to preserve their membership by identifying those who are *not* part of the group. By teasing and bullying those who are *outside* the group, teens broadcast to the world that they are *inside* the group. The thinking is, *If I can put you down, I can show everyone that you are out and I am in. I ridicule you to avoid being ridiculed myself.*

The leaders of these groups can become very powerful individuals. They can make or break someone else's social and school life. If a leader decides that someone is uncool, the other group members will go on the attack. The leader's display of power will solidify the group's standing and strengthen the leader's position. It can be difficult to belong to a group and resist the peer pressure to pick on someone else, because resisting might mean you will be picked on yourself. Many people go along with the terrorizing of others even though they know it to be wrong and secretly feel badly about it.

Naturally, it is very painful to be teased and bullied. Enduring this kind of behavior will lower self-esteem, increase insecurity and lead to anger. Because this anger is difficult to express, it can sometimes build and build until it finally explodes in an uncontrollable rage. In its most extreme form, it can lead to murderous acts like those committed at Columbine High. However, most teens will confine themselves to fantasies of revenge. These kinds of thoughts are normal—they do not mean that you are deranged, crazy or sick just for having them. Everyone has dark thoughts at times. However, we must never act out on these dark thoughts. When we do so, we destroy others and ultimately destroy ourselves. The Columbine killers may have gotten their revenge, but they needlessly destroyed a great many lives in the process, including their own.

It's normal to have an occasional fantasy about hurting ourselves or others, but it is unhealthy to dwell on such feelings. Doing this can compound your anger and reinforce the idea that it is okay to lash out in a rage. It is **never** right to act out in anger. If you have angry thoughts of revenge or retaliation, distract yourself from them by using the relaxation techniques we've discussed in this book. Turn off those angry emotions and turn on to more constructive thoughts.

If you feel your thoughts of doing harm to yourself or others might actually turn into actions, you must ask for help. Confide your thoughts with someone you trust and ask him/her to get you into counseling. Don't be afraid—a caring professional can help you to overcome your problem and banish those dark thoughts. Therapy will introduce some coping skills that are very similar to what we've already covered in this book.

There is some comfort in knowing that as we mature, concerns like popularity and acceptance become less important to us. However, until that maturity comes, adolescence can be a living hell. Over the years, I have worked with a great many teens who needed help coping with being bullied and teased. I can help you as well.

In order to help you cope with these issues, let's discuss some things about human functioning. The ability to learn is an important part of what makes us human. In fact, psychologists have devoted an entire field of study to how we learn and unlearn things. This field is called behaviorism. People who study behaviorism know that humans will repeat any behavior that is rewarded and reinforced. This instinct has survival value for our species. For example, babies learn that staying close to their mothers helps them to survive, so therefore they continue to stay close to their mothers. When the babies grow to become children and then adolescents, they learn new forms of behavior that help them satisfy their basic needs. We adopt and discard many different forms of behavior throughout our lives, depending on ever-changing circumstances and desires.

However, it is important to understand that the people who pick on others have *learned* this behavior and can also *unlearn* it. How can we accomplish this? First, we must discover what needs are being filled in the minds of the tormentors when they pick on someone. Why do they do it? The answer is obvious: attention. Tormentors pick on others in order to prove to themselves and everyone else that they are part of the "in" group. They put others down in order to lift themselves up. When a person responds to their teasing or bullying, this gives them the attention that they want. Such reactions reinforce their behavior and make it more likely that they'll target and provoke the person again in the future.

So, if you are being tormented and give your tormentors the attention they crave, they'll only come back for more.

Since attention is a powerful tool, it is important to use it wisely. When you are bullied or teased, don't give your tormentors any attention whatsoever. Act like a huge black hole that sucks in other people's negative energy but gives nothing back in return. This can be very difficult to do, because our natural instinct when provoked is to fight back. However, you must understand that this will not help the situation. If you do this, you will be giving your enemies exactly what they want. You don't want to help your enemies, do you? When tormentors pick on you, deny them the attention they crave. Focus on your own power—your power to remain unmoved by their taunting. Act as though these tormentors do not exist. Do not even honor them with a reaction, because they do not deserve it. They are not worth your time or attention.

The less attention you pay to your tormentors, the quicker they will leave you alone. Most likely, they'll move on to someone else in the hope of getting a reaction. Share your newfound power with others who can use it to defend themselves against bullies. In this way, the tormentors will fail.

Teen Anger Tips

- Teasing, bullying and tormenting are very commonplace among teens.
- Teens pick on one another in order to mask their own insecurities.
- Those who are "in" reinforce their positions by preying on those who are "out."
- It's normal to occasionally think about revenge and retaliation, but it's unhealthy to dwell on it.
- If you are seriously thinking about doing harm to yourself or others, ask for help.
- Paying attention to someone's behavior reinforces that behavior. Ignoring someone's behavior discourages that behavior.
- Your attention is a powerful tool. You can use it to control tormentors.
- Remember the power of the black hole. Suck the negative energy out of your tormentors by denying them the attention they crave.

chapter 20

Nonviolent Nonparticipation: Rules, Rule-makers and Anger

I got love for my brother but we can never go nowhere,
Unless we share with each other
Learn to see me as a brother instead of two distant strangers
And that's how it's supposed to be...
- Tupac Shakur, "Changes"

It's easy to understand what someone might mean by "violent partic-ipation," but it is more difficult to define "nonviolent nonparticipation." This is an idea I've learned from the philosophy of Dr. Martin Luther King, Jr., who used nonviolence as a strategy to win civil rights for African-Americans in the 1960s. Dr. King based his approach on the teachings of Mahatma Gandhi, who used a similar strategy to win India's independence from British colonial rule. Gandhi didn't want to force the British to leave India—he wanted to convince the British that leaving was the right thing to do. His achievement was remarkable. It was one of the few times in history a country won its independence without fighting a bloody war.

Dr. King and Gandhi were also brilliant in their abilities to persuade others to protest in nonviolent ways. When people feel oppressed, their natural tendency is to strike back with violence. Yet King and Gandhi taught their followers that they should counter oppression *without* becoming violent. They both thought that nonviolence was a far more effective tool to help them achieve their ends. Their philosophy may help you as well. Many teens feel oppressed by parental authority and want their independence. Some teens feel tyrannized by school personnel and some by the police. Some of these teens seek to overthrow this tyranny by rebelling. However, authority figures often feel threatened by such rebellions and they battle back. No one ever gets anywhere and all parties are frustrated. Isn't there a better way?

In family counseling, I teach teens to draw on the ideas of nonviolent protest. Violence won't get you what you want. Instead, use communication and negotiation to achieve your ends.

Teens tell their parents, "I want more freedom." Parents tell their teens, "We need to see some responsibility." Does this sound familiar? Perhaps you've reached this impasse with your own parents. How did you get around it? Perhaps anger and frustration led you to cop an attitude with your parents, sneak around behind their backs or openly defy them. Did any of these strategies ever work in the long run? More than likely, your parents responded by getting angry and cracking down on you. This caused you to fight and rebel once more and thus the cycle perpetuated itself. Rebellion led to a crackdown, which led to rebellion, which led to... This destructive cycle has to be broken.

The first step toward finding a nonviolent solution to the problem is identifying how the other side thinks and feels. Consider your parents' position for a moment. They've raised you from a little baby who needed their help and care in order to survive. Now their little baby is telling them that he or she is all grown up and wants to do things on his or her own. This is a hard thing for any parent to accept.

Once you identify your parents' concerns, you can try to meet those concerns and change their position. If your parents still see you as an infant, ask yourself how you might go about convincing them of your maturity. How can you get them to see you as an adult who deserves more freedom? Obviously, there are many different answers to this question. In the exercise which follows, you will brainstorm for some possible answers. One answer might be: "I'll call to let them know where I am or what I'm doing when I go out." Another might be: "Whenever I promise them I'll do something, I have to follow through and actually do it." Still another might be: "I'll show them I take my schoolwork seriously."

Teen Anger Exercise

What could you do to make your parents see you as more of an adult? Write down your ideas on the chart provided.

1. _____
   _____

2. _____
   _____

3. _____
   _____

4. _____
   _____

5. _____
   _____

If you understand your parents' concerns and take time to reassure them, they will give you more freedom. Again, this is the spirit of compromise: give up something in order to get something in return.

Now take your list to your parents as a peace offering. Promise them that you will follow each item on the list if they allow you more independence. Work out compromises on which everyone can agree. Then live up to your end of the agreement. The more responsibility you show your parents, the more they will trust you. The more they trust you, the more liberty they will allow you. Use the nonviolent techniques of Gandhi and King to confront the problems you have with your parents and to negotiate solutions.

One of my clients learned this technique very well. Marcia and her mother came to see me after Marcia was caught sneaking in the house at 3:00 A.M. on a school night. Her grades had been slipping and this incident was the last straw with Marcia's mom. A furious argument exploded between Marcia and her mother and in the end, Marcia was grounded indefinitely. When I first met with them and they began talking, I could see right away there was excessive anger and hostility between mother and daughter. Having divorced two years before, Marcia's mom was a single parent who worked a lot and could not always be home to be sure Marcia was staying out of trouble. Furthermore, it was clear that Marcia's mom would have great difficulty enforcing the indefinite grounding. I knew there had to be a better way, so I delved further into their relationship.

Her mother told me she was most concerned about Marcia's friends. As many parents do, her mom blamed Marcia's friends for the sneaking around, disobeying rules and Marcia's poor performance in school. She wanted to keep Marcia from seeing these friends. Marcia, naturally, was very upset by this and did not see her friends as the problem. In fact, Marcia said her friends were her only source of support and happiness. Marcia finally confessed that her grades started slipping and she started rebelling against the rules when her mom began seriously dating a new man, Jim. Before Jim came along, Marcia and her mom were actually quite close. Following the divorce, Marcia's mom focused all her time and energy on Marcia, but now that Jim was in their lives, Marcia felt her mom was abandoning her.

The teenager felt betrayed by her mom's new relationship. Marcia had been a good student and a responsible daughter helping out around the house and even cooking dinner. Mother and daughter had such a good relationship that there was little opportunity for conflict to arise and they didn't know how to handle it when it did.

Marcia's mom recognized that Marcia was basically a good kid and a responsible individual. She admitted that she grounded Marcia because she didn't know what else to do. I explained that the grounding only served to increase hostility and distance and would be detrimental to Marcia's development. I applauded mom for giving Marcia a strong foundation that would see the young woman through rough times ahead—better than any grounding would do. Marcia's mom agreed that the grounding was neither effective nor necessary. With that, the grounding was ended.

What Marcia and her mother had going for them was a strong bond; unfortunately, it was broken down by this conflict. I felt they needed to learn how to resolve their difficulties through compromise. With the ending of the grounding, Marcia's mom gave a lot of freedom back to Marcia. In return, Marcia said she'd be willing to introduce all her friends to her mom and call home to let her mom know where she was and what she was doing more often. This willingness alone helped to reassure Marcia's mom. The trustworthy daughter she had always known was still around.

Finally, I encouraged Marcia and her mom to keep the lines of communication open. By talking about issues and feelings, there was a lot less conflict between them. They talked about the divorce, mom's new relationship, Marcia's friends and school. Marcia and her mom quickly reached a much greater comfort level with each other and got their relationship back on track.

Another client, Billy, was sixteen when his father first brought him to meet me. Billy was very angry with his mother, however she never came to any sessions so I just worked with Billy and his dad.

With his father present, Billy described his mom as a strongly religious person. As a result, she had many strict rules and rigid expectations of Billy. Like any teenager, the older Billy got, the more freedom he desired. The conflicts between Billy and his mother were becoming more intense. Billy had begun not caring about school. As he said, "Why should I bother? Nothing I do ever pleases her."

Witnessing Billy expressing his feelings gave his father a newfound understanding of the boy's problems and he became more sympathetic toward Billy's position. Billy appreciated that his dad validated his concerns about his mom. Although Billy's dad did not want to take sides in this battle, at times he and Billy would share a moment to talk about things and his dad always promised to be there for him. They even shared some laughs from time to time about what a fanatic Billy's mom could be. This release was good for Billy and having the emotional support of his father was vital at this rough time in the teen's life.

I learned that Billy's mom was the disciplinarian. I suggested that Billy's father, who was usually more laid back and hands-off with the kids, take over as the primary disciplinarian for Billy. He wasn't too sure he wanted this responsibility, but I reminded him that the current situation just wasn't working for Billy and his mom. There was too much conflict, which resulted in self-defeating behavior. The strict discipline of his mother was driving Billy to act out more and more. I asked his father, "Who is being served by the strict rules and harsh discipline?" I asked the father to at least think about my insights. He went home and spoke to his wife. They agreed that my suggestion was a valid one. Billy's dad took over and in his more flexible, reasonable way, he and Billy were able to work things out. In fact, they worked quite well together. Billy even began getting along with his mother better.

Although Billy, Marcia and their parents went to a professional for help with their at-home conflicts, not everyone can do this. Furthermore, many conflicts can be resolved with some patience, communication and compromise. Remember, arguing, screaming and fighting will not lead to conflict resolution. Use nonviolent nonparticipation: think about the problem, come up with some solutions and discuss them calmly with your parents. Then agree on one. You'd be amazed how effective this can be!

Teen Anger Tips

- Practice nonviolent protest when you feel that authority figures are coming down on you.
- Instead of fighting, look for settlements and compromises.
- A common impasse occurs when teens want more freedom and parents want to see more responsibility. Use nonviolent methods to negotiate around this impasse.
- Put yourself in your parents' shoes. See things from their point of view.
- If you identify your parents' concerns, you can meet those concerns in order to get what you want.
- Give your parents a list of things you will do in order to earn their trust.
- Once you have made an agreement, stick to it.
- If you act responsibly, your parents will trust you. If they trust you, they will grant you more freedom.

Conclusion

You must be the change you wish to make in the world.
- Mahatma Gandhi

Congratulations! You've made it to the very end of the book. Now is the time to check to see what progress you've made so far.

As you apply the principles, techniques and exercises you learned in the book, take note of your new level of anger when dealing with others. You should see a change in how you communicate and react. One good way to track your ability to manage your anger and to see if you're making improvements in the way you react is to return to the two anger management tests in chapter 3 and take them a second time. Has your score improved? If not, don't be discouraged. It takes time and energy to change the way you feel and act. Furthermore, if you are surrounded by individuals who are not supportive or who constantly attempt to provoke other's anger, you will have to work extra hard and it may take longer to see results. Don't give up. As you change for the better and become more positive, you will find that positive people will be drawn to you and negative people will slip away. Pick up this book in three months or six months and take the tests again. In time you should see your scores improve.

I leave you at the end of this journey together with lifelong guidelines:

TRUTHFULNESS	"I tell the truth."
TRUSTWORTHINESS	"I am trustworthy."
ACTIVE LISTENING	"I actively listen with my ears, my eyes, my heart and my undivided attention."
NO PUT-DOWNS	"I never put down others."
PERSONAL BEST	"I always do my personal best."

Even when you have your anger firmly under control, there may be times when you need to refresh your memory about the concepts, exercises and skills covered in this book. When this happens, don't hesitate to return to the book for a quick review. Good luck!

Note to Parents

If you've bought this book for your teenager who is dealing with an anger problem, that is a good first step. However, it's not enough to force your teen to read this book alone. You should read it as well. If you want your teen to change, you must reassure him/her that he/she is not solely responsible for the problems at hand. Send the message that you will participate in the work of makings things better.

This book will instruct your adolescent to come to you with readings, exercises and new tools for the family to use. Encourage your child's emotional growth by participating.

As you and your teenager gain understanding and work through unresolved anger problems together, the bond between you will grow and strengthen.